OTHERWORLD

OTHERWORLD

Nine Tales of Wonder and Romance
from Medieval Ireland

LISA M. BITEL

OXFORD
UNIVERSITY PRESS

OXFORD
UNIVERSITY PRESS

Oxford University Press is a department of the University of Oxford. It furthers
the University's objective of excellence in research, scholarship, and education
by publishing worldwide. Oxford is a registered trade mark of Oxford University
Press in the UK and certain other countries.

Published in the United States of America by Oxford University Press
198 Madison Avenue, New York, NY 10016, United States of America.

Library of Congress Cataloging-in-Publication Data
Names: Bitel, Lisa M., 1958– author. | Joshaghani, Saba, illustrator.
Title: Otherworld : nine tales of wonder and romance from
medieval Ireland / Lisa M. Bitel.
Description: New York, NY : Oxford University Press, 2024. |
Includes bibliographical references and index.
Identifiers: LCCN 2024012971 (print) | LCCN 2024012972 (ebook) |
ISBN 9780197600610 (hardback) | ISBN 9780197600634 (epub)
Subjects: LCSH: Tales—Ireland—Adaptations. | Ireland—Social life and
customs—To 1500. | LCGFT: Fantasy fiction. | Mythological fiction. |
Paranormal fiction. | Romance fiction. | Poetry.
Classification: LCC PS3602.I8 O84 2024 (print) | LCC PS3602.I8 (ebook) |
DDC 818/.609—dc23/eng/20240530
LC record available at https://lccn.loc.gov/2024012971
LC ebook record available at https://lccn.loc.gov/2024012972

DOI: 10.1093/oso/9780197600610.001.0001

Printed by Sheridan Books, Inc., United States of America

To PCM, the man of my dreams

The teller shapes the tale and the tale returns the favor.

CONTENTS

LIST OF ILLUSTRATIONS

INTRODUCTION

ONCE UPON A TIME, A very few fortunate mortals found their way to the Otherworld—the early medieval Irish *síd*.

I will tell you some of their adventures in this book: nine enchanting tales from Ireland, all more than a thousand years old. These stories are about love and magic. They are about the boundaries between the present moment and the distant past, about parallel worlds and the strange borderlands between them. These tales inspired the earliest fairy tales as well as folktales that persist today, but they are sexier, funnier, and more exotic than all the tales that followed. They speak of the anguish of betrayal, and they celebrate enduring devotion. They probe the terrible choice between duty to family and duty to the heart. They boast of the impossible toils and triumphs of heroes and demigods and the unbelievable beauty of queens. They relish the shriek of the raven-winged war goddess and lament men's blood spilled on the muddy earth. Above all, these tales are about interracial love and desire shared by mortal humans and the supernatural *áes síde*, folk of the ancient Irish Otherworld.

If you are ready to read the tales, skip the rest of this introduction and hasten to the first page of the first story. If you want to prepare yourself for the Otherworld with some words on the history and literature of earlier Ireland, read on.

In the beginning, storytellers most likely sang some version of these stories for the pleasure of kings and their people, crowded around the hearths of royal halls on long winter nights. A respectable storyteller-poet (*fili*) was expected to know at least three hundred stories of all different kinds to keep his audience entertained for the whole dark, chilly, wet season.

Sometime before 700 CE, learned men in what we now call Christian "monasteries"—bustling settlements with a church or two, a market, craftsmen and women, family residences, houses for vowed men and priests, houses for vowed women, shrines, and sometimes *scriptoria* (libraries and writing rooms)—began to compose their own versions of the stories. We don't know whether they were inspired by tales they had heard, collaborated with traditional storytellers, or were storytellers themselves.

Whoever they were, they had learned how to read and write Latin and Irish. They scratched the tales with feather pens on vellum pages, squeezing them in between histories, saints' lives, laws, medical treatises, poetry, astronomy, and theological arguments. Books were expensive, the handwriting cramped, and pages not very pretty. One story ran into another with hardly a mark between them except perhaps an occasional capital letter. The scribes bound everything together in book form, rather like a modern reader or encyclopedia. Only the most prosperous religious communities could afford to maintain libraries and produce books, for a single volume required the skins of a small herd of sheep or calves for its folios. That is how valuable these tales of the Otherworld were to church-trained writers and their readers in eighth-century Ireland.

Ceist, as one of the scribes might write: a question. Why would devout churchmen spend both wealth and labor to preserve stories about love, lust, magic, violence, and a seemingly non-Christian Otherworld? By "Otherworld," I do not mean the idyllic plains of the afterlife in classical Greece and Rome, or Olympus of the gods, or the heaven and hell of biblical scriptures. I'm talking about an older supernatural world that was accessed by magic rather than death. An alternate reality.

The same scribe might answer, *Ní ansae:* not difficult to answer. Irish churchmen apparently did not consider ancient stories, properly contained in writing, to be contrary to their religion. Elsewhere in Christendom, intellectuals railed against pagan fables and poetry. Saint Augustine of Hippo urged his friends to avoid the theatre and gladiatorial games. Saint Jerome famously demanded to know what the Roman poet Horace had to do with Psalms in the Christian Psalter. In their minds, European mythologies (which they knew well) could only inspire wrong thoughts and sinful acts.

The Irish kept their ancient heritage alive in stories and histories, in the blend of old and new religious customs, and in their landscape of prehistoric burial mounds and royal hillforts sprinkled with churches. They recorded stories about places important to the pagan past; in turn, stories helped preserve the old monuments and sacral sites. They continued to bury their tribal kings in the ancient hills that had received previous generations of rulers. They held councils and mustered for war at these same hills, and inaugurated their kings atop the mounds. They erected saints' shrines in places that had once been dedicated to local spirits. Every ford, pass, river, hill, and plain had its origin story, and every story spoke of the ancient supernatural. Christian authors managed this heritage and the landscape by regarding the material environment historically. They even created a new genre of literature called *dindsenchas* to preserve the long history of place-names.

Still, in stories and place-names, the *síd* and its creatures remained present to medieval writers and audiences. The *síd* is and ever was, at once, an invisible Otherworld that parallels and preceded our reality; the creatures that abide there; and the places where mortals might try to enter the Otherworld, such as those ancient monuments and mounds, as well as certain caves, springs, lakes, lonely trees, and unseen islands far to the west of Ireland, among other spots. Portals to the *síd* led underground, but the Otherworld of early medieval tales was marvelously alight with constant sunshine on an otherwise rainy island. It shone with crystals and gemstones that decorated its sumptuous halls and its richly dressed people. Spring flowered all year round in the *síd*. Food and drink were bountiful and instantly available, and the music never ceased. No one labored for a living in the *síd*. The *áes side* took their pleasure by day and night. They were like humans, with appetites, character flaws, and desires. They had a social hierarchy and kept allegiance to their tribes. They married, had sex, and produced children. Yet they were also eternally youthful and perfectly beautiful. What is more, they were all golden-haired and had excellent teeth. Some of them could turn themselves into birds, as several stories in this volume attest. Mortals considered the fabulous *áes síde* to be a distinct race older than humans.

In stories, the *áes síde* entered the mortal world whenever they wished. They could move undetected among us. Sometimes they arrived in flashy chariots to challenge and recruit mortal warriors. They were beneficent or vengeful depending on individual personality and situation. They fought some humans and seduced others. They fell in love with us, and sometimes one of ours loved one of theirs. Even when mortals began to forget them—for in folklore, the supernatural races are always already departing the visible world—the *áes síde* could not resist interfering with human events.

In the later Middle Ages, French and English fairy tales turned the Otherworld into a magical kingdom with endless forests, doorless castles, knights both good and evil, and King Arthur. The women were still slim, pale, and golden-haired but, for the most part, far less lively and sexy than the women of Irish *síde* (pl. of *síd*). In Ireland, the written tradition of the *síd* continued for those who could read, while storytellers gradually reduced the Otherworld in size and complexity. No one has yet explained properly why and how this happened; likely, the politics of language, invasion, and occupation affected storytelling traditions during the early modern centuries. By the eighteenth and nineteenth centuries, dwellers in the Otherworld were usually tiny creatures, almost as small as English fairies, who feasted and danced by moonlight in the fields. They lured you into their circle and danced you to exhaustion. They stole human babies and left behind changelings. They abducted new brides. They messed about your house and farmyard. They occasionally took shape as humans lounging at the crossroads, or in regal processions following ordinary roads at midnight. The hideous banshee—*ban síde*, woman of the Otherworld—washed bloody garments in the river and keened to warn souls of approaching death.

The Otherworld remained nearby. The possibility of a mortal taking a supernatural lover or being courted by one of the *áes síde* never became impossible. Even in the twenty-first century, ordinary people blame the Good Folk for stealing things and preventing the building of houses and roads on their property. Still, proximity never promoted the liberal mixing of the races. Throughout the centuries, stories usually emphasized the trouble it caused. In early medieval tales, the mortal partner of a supernatural lover faced a terrible choice, for the *síd* was a superior place in all senses but one—it was not home. It did not include the mortal's family. Kinship was the basic organizational principle of medieval Irish life and law. A kinless individual was literally an out-law with no legal status, deprived of the affection, protections, and lands of family. Hence, an individual's decision to abandon their relatives for a lover from the *síd* (or even a spouse from a neighboring kingdom) meant total dependence upon that lover and their kin. Yet sometimes lovers grow cold, and what then? In medieval literature, Otherworldly folk came and went as they pleased, as stories in this collection show, but mortals were rarely able to resume their interrupted lives.

Still, the nine tales in this volume are about lovers who dared to cross boundaries of time, space, and race. Themes of mortality, the ephemerality of pleasure, the dangers of passion, and the perils of jealousy run like underground currents through early medieval stories of the *síd*. Some authors described the Otherworld in Christian terms, turning it into a sinless paradise. Other writers used the *síd* to mock Christian morality. Some tales emphasize the dangers of the Otherworld, especially at particular times of the year. For instance, on Samain eve (October 31), formerly a seasonal holiday commemorating the beginning of winter, doors to the Otherworld flew open and out came monsters, dead men, and demons, at least in some stories. Still other tales are historical in tone, involving supposedly real kings who ruled Ireland in the pre-Christian centuries, and who often encountered symbolic Otherworldly beauties, possibly meant to represent kingship. A few stories reached back to the origins of Ireland itself, depicting Otherworldly characters who tamed the wilderness for human habitation. The scholars of medieval Ireland were keen to establish their people's origin and locate it in the grander scheme of Creation history. In *The Courtship of Étaín*, for example, *síd*-folk clear landscapes of trees and swamps, teach humans how to build causeways over the bogs, and show them how to yoke their oxen properly.

The tales offer historical evidence for two worlds—I do not mean the *síd* and the real world, but instead pre-Christian, late Iron Age Ireland (around the first–fourth centuries, when most of the stories are set) and early medieval Ireland (roughly 650–900 CE), when the tales were written. The colorful details in the stories, such as what characters wore and ate, how their houses were furnished, or how they spoke to one another, reflect the world of medieval writers rather than life in the Iron Age. Like the sacred mounds of Ireland, early medieval stories accumulated layers of meaning over time. Contrary to what modern scholars once believed, medieval writers did not merely copy down, word for word, stories they heard at the fireside. Literate men (and it was probably all men) wrote their own renditions of traditional tales. Variants of many stories remain scattered in different manuscripts. Each time someone wrote a story into a new manuscript, the tale and its details shifted shape. Sometimes later copyists explained old-fashioned phrases or corrected episodes in the tales, and other times they wrote the stories afresh. Well into the seventeenth century, scribes rewrote the early tales in an Irish much changed from the medieval period, adding personal flourishes and leaving out bits that displeased them, or combining two tales into one.

Beginning in the nineteenth century, propelled by the same antiquarian urge that created folklorists like the Brothers Grimm, scholars searched Irish manuscripts for the oldest original versions of stories, using changes in the language to guide them. As academics toiled to transmit the ancient literature into printed books and academic journals, they often tried to fix up and piece together whole stories from the fragments scattered across multiple manuscripts, just as medieval copyists combined multiple versions of a single tale. Sometimes modern editors even "corrected" the language of stories to make it more archaic and authentic. When they translated the old stories into English, students of the language adhered strictly to the dictionary meanings of words and grammatical rules laid out by philologists. As a result, most twentieth- and early twenty-first-century translations are technically accurate, but their prose is often stiff or dreary. The wonders of the *síd* were lost to good grammar.

Although the tales have been translated repeatedly, they still resist it, and not only because they were passed down in a difficult language that few people today can read. For one thing, the stories include a lot of poetry written in the intricate rhymes and rhythms of medieval *filid*. Irish words do not rhyme in the way English words do—it is more like English near-rhyme. Alliteration is common. The rhythms vary, but syllable count is often crucial to a poem's struc-ture. I have translated the poetry with as much near-rhyme and alliteration as I could, but I was unable to imitate the formal structure of the verses. Whatever the bards sounded like when they burst into poetry, you will not hear it when you read these stories aloud. I have also tinkered with the prose, for example, altering verb tenses and voices, and sometimes substituting words that make more modern sense for translated archaisms. Where words are repetitive, I sometimes added variety. In the originals, every dialogue includes the tag "he said," "she said," or "they said," but I occasionally substituted "asked," "declared," or "cried," or I added adverbs.

Another major stumbling block in translating these stories is simply their age. They have come a long way, over twelve or thirteen centuries, via multiple manuscript and print editions and countless interpretations. As hard as historians try, we have lost too much of the Irish past to understand everything in these stories. Although archaeologists continue to discover more details about daily life in earlier Ireland, we can still only sketch the backdrop to these tales. As a trained historian, I can tell you that the thoughts and emotions of ordinary people, their desires, and dreams remain elusive. All of our texts came from the pens of a small learned class of churchmen. We have no idea what most people took for granted about their world, what they thought possible, and what was sheer nonsense. We almost never get their jokes.

A medieval writer did not need to explain his puns and jokes for readers. He did not halt the narrative to elaborate on aspects of the ordinary, visible world. Scribes never explained, for example, that Irish houses of the early medieval period typically consisted of one large round room with a hearth in the middle, built of wattle and mud with a thatched roof, set in a fenced enclosure. They did not include footnotes rehearsing how women cooked at the hearth set in the middle of the house, using big iron pots for stews and laying bread to bake on the hot stones; or that those same women were completely disenfranchised by the legal system; or how marriage was a usually a loveless contract made between two families; or that life expectancies were short and infant mortality high. Medieval authors never mentioned that when food ran short, everyone starved; or that the heroic battles rendered so gloriously in old stories were destructive and tragic for noncombatants. Nor did storytellers repeat everything that everyone already knew about the *síd*.

For medieval audiences, the pleasure of a tale came not only from the bard or writer's artistry, shared with a crowd of listeners or other readers, but also from familiarity with the material. The Irish stories were interrelated. Consider the most famous English-language medieval epic, *Beowulf*. It exists in isolation from the rest of medieval English literature because similar and related epics have been lost over time. In Irish stories, which are plentiful by comparison, characters moved between tales, one plot led to another, and authors slyly referred to events in other narratives. The hero of one story turned up as a bit player in another. Audiences could anticipate unfolding storylines because they knew what had happened to characters before and after a particular tale. They noticed when a storyteller changed or abbreviated an episode, or left out a poem. They understood that characters in some stories went by different names in other tales, and that some heroic protagonists had once, perhaps, been gods. Audiences also recognized clues to the Otherworld in the tales—the astounding beauty of characters, their dress, even the color of their cloaks and hair signaled creatures from the *síd*. Writers used certain well-known phrases to announce the appearance and disappearance of creatures from the *síd*.

What is more, medieval audiences accepted contradictory details and multiple endings to a tale. For instance, the writer of *The Sickbed of Cú Chulainn or the Only Jealousy of Emer* called his heroine Eithne for the first half of the tale and Emer in the second half, probably because the particular version of the story that survived was a mash-up of pieces found in different manuscripts or recounted by various storytellers. Medieval audiences grasped that stories were always changing and often in tension with each other. They knew that storytellers told tales in their own peculiar ways. They also got the jokes.

Although this book contains only nine tales, more stories remain to us from Ireland than anywhere else in medieval Europe before 1000 CE. Modern academics have tidily sorted most of these linked tales into four literary cycles. The Mythological Cycle consists of tales about the immortal inhabitants of Ireland before the coming of Noah's descendants, that is, the Túatha Dé (Danann) or the Tribes of the Gods or of the Goddess (Danu). The larger-than-life figures in these stories are the closest to a pre-Christian pantheon we have found for Ireland. The second, the Ulster Cycle, treats Ireland's major medieval epic, the *Táin Bó Cúailnge* (*Cattle-Raid of Cúailnge*), and its "pre-tales" or *rem-scéla*. The latter are stories that help explain events in the larger epic. The *Táin* has been ably and poetically translated several times and also rendered visually in animated short films and graphic novels. Several tales in this book featuring the hero Cú Chulainn come from that cycle. The third, the King Cycle, treats semi-historical tales about Ireland's earliest rulers. Finally, stories of the *fian*, the mercenary band led by Finn Mac Cúmhaill that roamed the woods and wilderness, make up the Fenian Cycle. The tales here come from all but the Fenian Cycle, most of whose texts were written later in the Middle Ages. All the stories here were originally written before 1000 CE, some of them three or four centuries earlier. The problem with this modern cyclical scheme is that many tales seem to belong to more than one cycle. Characters refuse to stay put in a single story, cycle, or literary genre. The heroes of king-tales, for example, turn up in the monastic annals, which record dates of battles and the deaths of historical figures. Members of the Túatha Dé appear in legal material and in tales of saints. Writers and audiences of earlier Ireland did not organize their stories in cycles but instead categorized tales according to types. They made lists of the many stories that every good bard had to know, sorted by plot: abductions, elopements, courtships, death tales, destructions, voyages, adventures, and loads more. The tales in this volume include courtships (*Tochmarca*), dreams (always of an Otherworldly figure—*Aislingi*), and adventures (specifically in the Otherworld—*Echtrai*), as well as one death (*Aided*) and one sickness or sickbed (*Serglige*), although the latter could easily be called an *Echtra*.

The tale-types, like the medieval Irish tales themselves, are by nature fluid and interactive, like the recited stories that inspired them. When a professional raconteur recites a tale, they interact with their audience to explain a few things and help the tale along. While telling one version of a story, they might pause to mention variants of an episode, or multiple paths that a story could take. A burst of poetry might halt the action but deepen the meaning of a plot twist, like a show tune erupting in a Broadway musical. People often interrupt storytellers with questions, comments, applause, and sometimes rude noises. In manuscripts, scribes also occasionally interrupted the main narrative to remind readers of alternative names for characters, to locate a setting, or to suggest what happened to a figure that disappeared from a tale. Later copyists offered their own opinions and corrections between the lines. Once in a while, a copyist scraped away something he didn't like and rewrote the passage.

Another thing about medieval texts: they often overflow with seemingly repetitive and annoying details that slow the plot, such as long descriptions of the characters' physical appearance or the virtues of their horses. These descriptive passages must have been favorites for medieval audiences, though, as they occur in almost all the stories. They offered storytellers and writers a chance to show off their erudition and their talent for poetry and wordplay. Medieval authors invented adjectives in order to augment their lengthy accounts of heroes' facial features and handsome bodies, the quality and appearance of their horses, and their formidable weaponry—there simply were not enough existing words for blond hair, excellent steeds, and bloodied swords. How many ways can you say "war-like" or "beautiful"? How many synonyms exist for "red"? In my translations, I sometimes shortened these disquisitions because I ran out of English equivalents.

Equally wordy passages describing places on the Irish landscape also demonstrated the writers' expertise and education. The stories were anchored to the hills and rivers and forts that everyone once recognized. Even worse, sometimes characters spoke in elaborate riddling sentences which some character then explicated at length. Hence, while some episodes in the tales trot with snappy dialogue, other episodes loiter among puns, poetry, and adjectives. The prose may thunder toward combat or sidle in erotic directions, brusquely render a tryst or malinger in what seem like unnecessary directions to local burial mounds.

I spent two years completing new translations of these nine medieval stories. All of the stories have been translated before, mostly by scholars far more expert at reading Old and Middle Irish. Then I did what every previous bard, author, editor, and translator did by making my own versions, aiming for a historically contextual feel of the tales rather than precise, diplomatic translations. Above all, I aimed to make this a storybook, not a classroom reader. I grew up immersed in the fairy stories written by the Brothers Grimm and Andrew Lang before I graduated to Tolkien's neo-medieval epic and other modern fantasies, and I learned that storytellers do not relegate their interventions to footnotes. Much like medieval storytellers and scribes, but unlike modern academic translators, I have integrated my explanations and interpretations into the stories themselves. If characters have a significant backstory, or if they do puzzling things in a tale, or if a place or object has special resonance in the literature or history, I explain it to my readers. I have relied on other medieval texts, including other stories but also laws, annals, and religious documents, for these interpolations. Sometimes I point out themes and tropes that link these nine tales or bind them to texts beyond this volume. My additions are meant to suggest the assumptions of medieval audiences and to offer some of the familiarity with the stories felt by earlier audiences.

I also offer opinions. I direct questions to the audience. I expect that readers will discern my voice within the tales, but if not, I have listed other translations and editions of the texts in the Afterwords of this book, along with a few pertinent literary analyses and readings in medieval Irish history, so that you can compare my interpretations to others. It is not meant as a comprehensive scholarly bibliography, merely a list of suggestions.

Splendid and evocative illustrations by Saba Joshaghani grace this book. They, too, retell and enhance the tales. They bring the characters and the landscape to life. They make the *síd* visible. Text and images work together to fill in the blanks of literary conventions and historical silences.

A final note before we plunge into the stories: I use the early medieval names of places and characters. Although I hope to bring the magic of these stories to modern readers, I also feel that it is important to remind ourselves that visiting the past is like visiting an exotic island. The places in these stories are not as easily known as we might presume, even if some of the plots seem universally meaningful. So Tara is Temair, the Boyne River is Bóinn, Ireland/Éire is Ériu, and so forth. "Pagan" is how they thought of people who were not Christians. "Girls" could mean females between the ages of thirteen and ninety.

Guides to Irish place-names are included in the list of readings.

Now follow me, if you dare, into the *síd*. Watch your step.

"As she fled the druid's chanting, she threw an apple to Connlae."

THE FIRST TALE

Echtra Chonnlai—The Adventure of Connlae

THIS IS THE OLDEST EXISTING story about love and the Irish Otherworld. It was probably written around 700 CE, although the action took place five centuries earlier, when King Conn of the Hundred Battles reigned over pagan Ériu. Or so said the medieval scholars. By 700, most Irish called themselves Christians.

Its hero, Connlae, has little to say. Most of the dialogue is among his father, Conn, the druid Coran, and a mysterious nameless beauty who chants poetry to the bemused Connlae. Druids appear in many of the tales as advisers and diviners of kings. In saints' lives they were magicians who could change the weather and bring darkness over the land, but in the tales druids are mostly wise, friendly old men who made ambiguous predictions.

As for the Otherworldly beauty in this story, her purpose seems clear, but her identity less so, for she remains unseen to all but Connlae. Is she illusion or reality? Metaphor or history? The question plagues many tales about the Otherworld. This brief tale is not as straightforward as it might at first seem. It has too many puns and double meanings to be simple. It is not a very exciting tale, and it may seem there is not much to discuss in it, but as you will see, it leads the way to the Otherworld.

One day Connlae Rúad (the Ruddy), son of Conn Cétchathach (of the Hundred Battles), was standing next to his father on the top of the hill at Uisnech, in the very center of Ériu, when he saw a woman in unusual clothing approaching.

He asked her, "Where have you come from, unearthly woman?"

She responded:

I have come from Lands of the Living,
where there's no death, no sin, no guilt.
We have feasts without any effort,
Consent without any strife.
In utter peace we live, we are called
the People of Peace, the áes síde.

The woman punned, for *síd* in old times was a word for "peace" as well as a word for the Otherworld.

"Whom are you addressing?" asked Conn Cétchathach, for no one could see the woman except Connlae.

The woman replied,

He is speaking to a lovely young Lady
Who does not expect death or age.
I have always loved Connlae the Ruddy.
I summon Connlae to The Plain of Delights
Where Bóadag the Immortal reigns.
No woe or weeping exists in his land
Since that king began to rule.

Come with me, O Connlae Ruad,
You with the red-freckled neck,
Golden curls above a blushing face,
Your kingly appearance marks you.
If you come with me, your youth will not wither
Until the dreamed-of Doomsday.

Everyone heard the woman, but none could see her. Conn the king said to Coran the druid,

I beseech you, O Coran
Of great song and skill,
An undue demand is being made,
Beyond my wisdom,
Beyond my power,
As has never afflicted me
Since I began to rule.
Canny phantoms constrain me,
While snatching my splendid son,
Taking him from my royal hand
with the wily spells of women.

The druid then chanted protective magic over the place where the woman stood, so that her voice could not be heard, and so that Connlae could no longer see the woman. As she fled the druid's chanting, she threw an apple to Connlae.

For a whole month, Connlae went without eating or drinking, consuming nothing but the apple. Yet the apple never diminished, always remaining whole, no matter how much he ate of it.

Desire for the woman in his vision seized Connlae.

One day, when the month of her banishment was over, Connlae was standing next to his father in the Plain of Arcommin. He saw the same woman coming toward him. She challenged him:

An exalted seat
In which Connlae sits
Among the short-lived, almost-dead
Who await desperate ends.
The ever-living invite you!
You are a champion to the sea folk
Who observe you every day
In the assemblies of your homeland
Among your familiar dear ones.

When King Conn Cétchathach heard the woman's voice, he ordered his household, "Call the druid to me. I see she was released from his spell today."

Then the woman addressed him,

O Conn of the Hundred Battles,
Do not adhere to druidry, for
It is only a little while until
A righteous man, sent by the Great High-King,
With plenty of praiseworthy followers,
Will come for your judgements.
His law will soon fall upon you,
It will spoil the spells of mistaught druids
Before the dark and deceitful devil.

King Conn thought it strange that Connlae had spoken to no one until the woman appeared again. "Have the woman's words taken your mind, Connlae?" he asked.

Connlae finally spoke to his father. "This is not easy for me, for I love my people, but desire for the woman overwhelms me."
The woman said,

I shall free you from demands.
You long to sail to sea.

We may get there in my crystal ship,
We may reach the síd of Bóadag.

There is yet another land
That may not be the nearest.

I see the sun is sinking.
Though far, we'll land before dark.

That land brings joy and gladness
To the mind of each it snares.

There is no tribe there but one,
A tribe of women and girls.

Then Connlae suddenly leapt away from his father and the druid, and landed safely in the crystal-clear ship.
King Conn and the druid watched the ship as far as their eyes could follow.
The couple went to sea and was never seen again.

Now, some say that this story explains why Art, another son of Conn Cétchathach, was called "Art Alone," for after Conn disappeared, Art was brotherless. Others insist that Connlae and yet another brother named Crinda were slain by their enemies, thus leaving Art Alone, and had nothing to do with beauties from the *síd*.

Scholars and priests insist that this tale of Otherworldly seduction is not about Connlae's escape to the *síd*. They insist that it is an allegory about a young man who sheds his earthly concerns and journeys with an angel to Paradise, that place of peace, plenty, and purity. Still, what did it matter to Art the Lonely if Bóadag's kingdom and the Land of Women were metaphors for heaven, or if Connlae's ship was headed for a metaphorical kingdom rather than an island in the far seas? Either way, Connlae abandoned his kin to follow his yearning heart and left Art Alone. Except for their father and his druid, of course.

"My wife is the best at pouring drink in all Ériu. I shall recognize her pouring."

THE SECOND TALE

Tochmarc Étaíne—The Courtship of Étaín

IT WAS ÓENGUS THE MAC Óc who started the trouble in this tale, in his typically fearless fashion, although he was still just a lad at the time. The Mac Óc's impertinent deeds and arrogant temperament were the nut from which grew a hardy tree, its many branches bearing scenes of passion, loss, and wonders of the *síd*. Its roots sank into the earth when the Túatha Dé still ruled Ériu, and its leaves touched the sky when mortals came to the island. Noah's descendants chased the *áes síde* underground, as historians will tell you.

The tale of Étaín, Midir, and the Mac Óc sings of a love whose sting could fell a warrior. A love that conquered unbearable centuries of separation. A love that sneaked behind men's backs. It tells of arrogant kings who bought and sold women, and who could not discern one beauty from another. It recalls men who threw unwanted girls into pits with hungry beasts. It sets kings of the Otherworld against mortal rulers in games of smooth hustling and legal trickery, impossible tasks and inescapable boons, boasts, and bargains.

It speaks for a woman who could not speak for herself or control her own future. Étaín sits quietly at the heart of this tale, like the burl of an ancient oak. Fair Étaín, the object of desire and jealousy, Étaín of the long golden tresses with her lovers and husbands, Étaín shamed and abandoned, Étaín restored and reborn, who finally spoke up for herself and unfurled her wings. Étaín who could turn a man into a king.

Midir learned to love Étaín, but it took a thousand years of patience and all his wits to win her back.

The tale is three-pronged, like a hero's spear, but it all began with the Mac Óc.

Long ago, a great king named Eochaid Ollathar ruled the Túatha Dé. Ollathar means All Father. To his people he was indeed a good father. They also called him the Dagda because he governed the weather and protected the harvests. Dagda means the Good God.

The lords and ladies of the Túatha Dé took many names and shapes.

The Dagda moved from one of his halls to another throughout the seasons, though he lived much of the time at Uisnech in the very middle of Ériu. He often visited Brug na Bóinne, which sits between the solemn mounds at Dubad and Cnóbha. The river Bóinn flows eastward past the Brug. It begins in the bogs, cuts northward through green vales and pastures where tall grasses wave, wends through dark damp woods, and rushes over stones that clack together. It empties into the sea near Droichet Átha, but that place did not exist in the most ancient times.

The Dagda first followed that river inland when he was a war-leader of the Túatha Dé. His people came from the north in storm-clouds of magic to settle in Ériu. First, though, they had to contend with the existing lords of the island, the mysterious Fomoire, the watermen, who were at the time still warring with another monstrous race, the Fir Bolg. After many adventures, the triumphant Túatha Dé subdued the others and made their way to the very womb of Ériu, where they built their great halls on the mounds at Brug na Bóinne. Some say their rulers flourished for a thousand years and more. Their halls are long gone, but the mounds still rise beside the Bóinn's banks. Many great kings found their rest beneath those mounds.

So, long ago, Eochaid Ollathar the Dagda had his eye on a certain Eithne, wife of Elcmar of the Brug. Elcmar was Eochaid Ollathar's chief steward. Eithne had another name, too: Boand, after the great river. It may be, as other tales say, that when the river itself took womanly form, she became Boand. Her hall was called after her, Brug na Bóinne. Some say that Boand's Hall was the first house ever built in Ériu. Others, though, point to far older places out west, where caves and crude slabs of rock tipped together served as shelter for older deities and forgotten ancestors.

For now, we shall call her Boand and him Dagda. Dagda wanted Boand. He had watched her at feasts and games, and in the solemn crowds that gathered to hear his judgments. He had spied her slipping into the river in the moonlight. He had heard of her skills at magic and her talents for pouring drink, an important duty for the wife of a ruler. Her skills as a lover were obvious to him. Her beauty, in his eyes, was unsurpassed.

What woman would turn him down? Granted, he was a giant of a man with a long unruly beard. His clothes never fit properly. He was always hungry—he could consume a whole cauldron full of porridge. Still, he was well-intentioned and wise, and he ruled the Túatha Dé. He was skilled in many arts. He was a druid. He had a cauldron always full enough for a feast. He carried a massive club; one side crushed enemy heads, while a touch of the other side could resurrect a man. He also owned an oaken harp whose spellcasting voice set the pace of the seasons and ordered the minds and hearts of the Dagda's people.

But Boand feared the wrathful power of her husband, Elcmar. If he discovered her tryst with the Dagda, Elcmar would punish her, not by beating or starving her as some husbands did to their wives, but with magic. He would challenge the Dagda with spells and spears. After all, the man's name meant Spiteful.

Cunning Eochaid Ollathar, the Dagda, had his own special powers. He sent his man Elcmar on an official visit to the hall of Bres son of Elatha, in the north at Mag nInis. Bres had once been king of the Túatha Dé. His mother was one of them, but his father, Elatha, came from the Fomoire. The Túatha Dé chose Bres to rule them because they believed he could make peace between the two peoples. Bres was gorgeous to look at—after his birth, his name was used as the word for everything beautiful: Bres this, Bres that. His rule was less than perfect, though. He forced the folk of the Túatha to labor like slaves for the Fomoire in exchange for a promise of peace. Bres's judgment was not sound. That is a dangerous trait in a king, so the Túatha brought him down.

When Elcmar left the Brug to head north on his mission, he stepped out the door into a fog of enchantment. The Dagda wove masterful charms around Elcmar to delay the steward's return. He prevented the night from falling upon Elcmar. He relieved Elcmar of hunger and thirst and kept him busy with important duties, so that nine months passed though they seemed to Elcmar a single day.

The Dagda and Boand lay together.

We know no more about it, except that Boand conceived a child and nine months later delivered a son that she named Óengus. She entrusted the baby to the Dagda while she recovered. By the time Elcmar returned home, she was whole and hale, and there was no evidence that Boand had trysted with the Dagda, at least, not at the Brug. Even among the god-people, adulterers were cautious.

The Dagda sent the boy to be fostered by Midir, who lived nearby at Brí Léith in Tethbae. Midir may have been one of the Dagda's many sons, although some poets argue that he was the son of Induí, king of the northern horse-breeders. This is certain: Midir was a shrewd student of rules and laws. He knew all the ways around them. He could sense men's motives, play on their greed and desire, and twist the words that fell from their lips, although he was no arbiter of women, as it turns out.

Midir was happy to take Óengus from the Dagda, raise him, and set the boy loose among his other fosterlings. Óengus spent nine years with Midir learning masculine skills. Three fifties of lads from across Ériu trained and competed on the vast green playing field before Midir's house. Three fifties of noble girls perched at the edge of the green, pretending to embroider and gossiping as they watched the lads.

Midir loved Óengus more than any of his fosterlings because the boy was handsome and his family more distinguished than the lot. Foster father and foster son were mutually loyal for life. At least, that was how it was supposed to be, according to the laws.

During his time at Brí Léith, Óengus earned his nickname. They called him Óengus mac ind Óg or the Mac

Óc—the Young Lad—because of something his mother said: "Young is the Lad conceived at the start of day and born before evening." It was amusing to those few who knew the secret of his conception.

Mac Óc led Midir's boy-troop, which practiced martial skills and rough games every day in hopes of becoming great warriors like Midir and the Dagda. They raced and tumbled and sported with spears on the green. They used their slings to bring down birds and hares. They played hurley with weighty sticks and heavy round stones, and showed no mercy to their opponents. It was no game without blood.

One day, Óengus fell into an argument with Tríath son of Febal (or son of Gobar, as others say) of the Fir Bolg. Tríath was the other leader of the boy pack. He, too, was a fosterling of Midir, although he came of a conquered people.

Óengus refused to speak to Tríath because of his race. He declared, "It galls me that a slave's son should speak to me." He was rude and offensive, but like other young ones of the Túatha Dé, Óengus had been taught that the Fir Bolg were a lesser people. Also, Óengus believed that Midir was his father and that he, the Mac Óc, would inherit the kingdom of Brí Léith. He did not yet know about his tie to the Dagda.

Tríath knew better. He smirked at Óengus the Mac Óc and responded, "It's just as bad when a servant who doesn't even know his own mother or father tries to speak to me."

Óengus went wailing and grieving to Midir after Tríath shamed him.

Midir observed his fosterling with his usual calm. "What is it?" he asked.

"Tríath rebuked me. He taunted me to my face that I have no mother or father."

"False," said Midir, much as a lawgiver might judge a plea.

"Answer me then: who is my mother and who is my father?" Óengus demanded.

"Easy. Eochaid Ollathar is your father. He is the Dagda, king of the Túatha Dé. Eithne, wife of Elcmar of the Brug, is your mother. She is called Boand. I raised you without Elcmar knowing, so that he would not learn about your secret making."

Óengus scowled. "Come with me to visit Eochaid Ollathar and make him admit that he is my father, so that I will no longer be unnamed, and so the Fir Bolg will stop mocking me."

The Mac Óc had learned from Midir how to argue. He got his politics from the fierce play on the green. He began to understand just how much respect was due every different man and woman. He also knew that kings must establish their sons and that Midir must oblige him out of loyalty and duty to his foster son.

So Midir went with his fosterling to speak with Eochaid Ollathar at Uisnech. Eochaid would sometimes stay a whole year in Tech nEchach, the House of Eochaid, because it was equidistant from the south, north, east, and west of Ériu. The king sat in the middle of his island.

They found Eochaid the Dagda holding court. His warriors lounged about the hall, warming themselves by the fire in its center, and roaring for more to eat and drink. Serving women brought haunches of roasted meat and vats of beer.

Midir knew how best to present the problem of Óengus. He hailed the king, asking that Eochaid step aside to speak privately with the boy.

"What is the request of this fine young man before me?" asked Eochaid.

Midir replied in the same formal speech. "He requests lawful acknowledgment by his father and asks for the property that is his due," he said. "It is not right that your son has no lands of his own, given that you are king of Ériu." Midir himself had considerable property, as they all knew.

"He is welcome," said Eochaid, assessing both man and lad. "He is my son. He shall have land, but," the Dagda said thoughtfully, "the territory I would give him is not unoccupied at the moment."

"What territory?" asked Midir.

"The Brug north of the river Bóinn."

"Who occupies it?" inquired Midir, although he knew the answer.

"Elcmar is there now," Eochaid said, "and I do not wish to offend him again."

Midir understood. The Dagda could hardly expel his steward Elcmar and then give the same hall to his bastard child by Elcmar's wife. Boand's fear of Elcmar made the Dagda cautious. Still, the Mac Óc had to receive property from his father in order to be recognized as a noble warrior. A man without a hall and herds was no man at all.

"A question then. What advice would you give to this lad?" asked Midir.

"I have this to say to him," Eochaid answered. "On the solemn day of Samain at the end of autumn, he should go to Brug na Bóinne—and go armed. As everyone knows, that is a special day of peace and comradeship among the men of Ériu, when no man shows hatred to another. They will pile their weapons at the gate when they enter the Brug. Elcmar will preside over his assembly place, Cnoc Síde at the Brug, unarmed except for a forked branch of white hazel in his hand, wearing his cloak caught by a gold brooch. There will be three fifties of young warriors competing before him on the playing field, hoping for his praise. On that day, Óengus should go to Elcmar and threaten to kill him."

Midir and the Mac Óc knew it was a dishonorable plan. It could work.

"Best not to kill him, though, so long as he promises to grant your request," added the Dagda. "Óengus should demand to be king for a day and a night in the Brug. After that day and night, the lad must refuse to hand back the Brug and its lands. Elcmar will demand that the matter be settled at my court. He will think I support him because he is my man and I have given him a hall. When Elcmar brings the case to me, Óengus must argue that he gained the land in return for sparing Elcmar's life. He demanded to hold Elcmar's territory for a day and a night." Dagda grinned. "Then you must remind Elcmar of the old saying: 'It is in days and nights that the world goes on.'" For in the old language, "a day and a night" is the same "day and night."

Even Midir, who had a devious legal mind, would not have proposed the low trick of the Dagda.

Midir had to explain the riddle to the Mac Óc as they returned home.

At the next Samain, when dark winter descends with its endless nights and the Otherworld opens to our world, Óengus armed himself with spear and shield as Eochaid Ollathar had recommended and went to the Brug. It was exactly as the Dagda had predicted: Men left their weapons behind and drank together amiably. Elcmar presided without his sword and shield, clad in a cloak with shiny gold brooch, carrying only a forked wand of white hazel. The wand signified his unearthly powers, but it did not offer much protection.

The Mac Óc did as advised, although it defied custom. He rushed sword-first into the hall and threatened Elcmar. In return for sparing his life, Elcmar allowed Óengus to rule the Brug for a day and a night. Elcmar left the hall scowling while the Mac Óc presided over his territory. All of Elcmar's people obeyed him as their king.

Elcmar came the next day to reclaim his hall and land and people and animals from the Mac Óc, but the lad menaced Elcmar even more viciously. The Mac Óc announced that he would not give up the Brug until the matter was brought to Eochaid Ollathar, the Dagda, who would proclaim his decision before the men of Ériu. Elcmar agreed, for he was certain that Eochaid Ollathar would favor his complaint, return the Brug to him, and rid them of the imp Mac Óc.

All of them proceeded to Tech nEchach, where they appealed to the Dagda.

The Dagda laid out a settlement for each man according to his deeds and merit in the matter. "This lad henceforth holds the land, as he claims. That is just," decreed the Dagda, "for Elcmar submitted to Óengus and released his kingdom when he was threatened on the day of peace and amity."

To the furious Elcmar he added, "You yielded your position and acknowledged his superiority because you cared more for your life than your land." The Dagda gave Elcmar a gracious smile. "Never mind, you shall have other lands from me, no less valuable than the Brug."

"What is the place?" demanded Elcmar.

"Cleitech," said the Dagda, "with the three estates around it. Your boy-troop will spend every day in the plain before the Brug at their brutal games, and you shall reap the fruits of the river. It will feed you well."

You would think that Elcmar was already reaping fruits of the Bóinn, given that he was married to her. Perhaps she kept other secrets from her formidable mate. Or maybe other storytellers forgot that Eithne had another name. Maybe the Dagda made them forget.

"Agreed," said Elcmar, "let it be done thus." But his eyes followed the Mac Óc out the hall.

Elcmar moved to Cleitech and built a fort there.

The Mac Óc went to live in the Brug on his newly acquired lands.

One year later, Midir visited his foster son at the Brug. It was Samain again, and he found the Mac Óc atop the mound of the Síd in Broga (the *síd* of the Brug). That was the best place for a holiday assembly. The air was crisp with the coming winter and thick with unpredictable magic.

Two boy-troops played before Óengus on the green field of the Brug. One gang was from the Brug, the other from Elcmar's hall. From the hill, Midir and Óengus could see Elcmar upon his mound at Cleitech, a long walk to the south, watching the field of play.

A fight broke out among the lads.

"Do not move," Midir ordered the Mac Óc, "lest Elcmar come down among the lads on the field and make things worse. I will go myself to separate them."

Midir dove into the fray. It was difficult even for him, the smooth-tongued adjudicator, to separate the fractious lads.

While he was still trying to break up the fight, someone shot a holly dart that struck Midir square in the face and tore out one of his eyeballs.

Midir stalked back to the Mac Óc with the wet raw eyeball clasped in his fist. Blood dripped from his eyehole to his hand, from his hand to the land. He said bitterly, "I should never have come here to be blemished and shamed. Now I cannot gaze on the lands I am visiting, nor will I see again the lands that I left behind at Brí Léith." He said that because, according to tradition, a disfigured warrior could not rule a kingdom, but must yield his rule to an uninjured lord. You might say that Elcmar, too, was blemished by his fear, which is why he lost the Brug to the Mac Óc.

"It shall not be so," declared the Mac Óc, as a lawgiver might say to a petitioner, for Óengus knew that fosterlings owed a great debt to the ones who raised them. "I will go to Dían Cecht, the famous healer of the Túatha Dé, and fetch him to you. You will have your land back and you will be able to view my land, and your eye will be healed without any lasting flaw or dishonor."

So Mac Óc went to find Dían Cecht. Not only was the man a wondrous healer, he was also another son of the Dagda. He could cure any wound, even mortal ones, excepting only cases of decapitation and broken spines. He understood the problem of disfigurement. He had once crafted a silver arm for Nuadu, another king of the Túatha Dé, after Nuadu lost his fleshy arm in battle with the Fomoire. Then Nuadu was called Nuadu Airgetlam: Silverhand.

"Would you come with me to the Brug," asked Mac Óc, "to fix my foster father who was injured on the day of Samain?" Dían Cecht agreed and came to treat Midir. Soon after, Midir was healthy and as handsome as ever.

"My visit is a good one now," Midir admitted, "since I am healed and I have no scars."

"That is the truth," agreed the Mac Óc, solemn as a judge.

"Stay here until the end of the year," he pleaded, "so that you may review my warrior troop and my people and my household and my domain."

Perhaps it had occurred to the lad that all his possessions had come to him thanks to Midir, who had taken him to the Dagda to win the Brug from Elcmar.

Still Midir resisted. "I shall not stay," he declared, "unless I receive legal compensation for my injured honor and the painful wound to my face." It was, after all, the law.

"What kind of compensation?" wondered the Mac Óc. He had already brought Dían Cecht to heal his foster father and made Midir welcome in his hall.

"Not difficult. I want a chariot worth seven slave women," said Midir as casually as ever, "and a cloak suitable for someone of my status." Óengus nodded at the request, which was reasonable and not hard to fulfill.

But Midir was not finished. A small smile flickered on his face. "And the fairest woman in Ériu for my own."

"I have the chariot and cloak," said the Mac Óc.

Midir stood with arms crossed. "The woman whose shapeliness surpasses that of all the women of Ériu."

Óengus should have guessed what Midir was up to. "Where is she?" he asked.

"She is in Ulaid," said Midir. "Étaín Echraide—Étaín the Horsewoman—daughter of Ailill, king of the northeast of Ériu. She is the loveliest, most courteous, and virtuous woman in Ériu."

So the Mac Óc went off on his quest to Mag nInis, to the house of Ailill, king of the northeast. That, by the by, is the same region where Elcmar headed on his nine-month journey to the hall of Bres. Also the region that King Dichu offered to Saint Pátraic for building his church, many ages later—but that is another story.

They welcomed Mac Óc there. He feasted and drank with them for three nights. Attractive women were all over the place, serving drink, bringing meat, laughing and singing. Óengus probably thought about getting one of his own.

At last Óengus declared his purpose: he had come to ask for Étaín.

The girl was not present in the hall, but the news reached her that a man of the Túatha Dé was asking to marry her. No one mentioned Midir.

King Ailill shook his head. "I will not give her to you because I cannot benefit from the arrangement. The status of your people is too elevated and your power too great, not to mention that of your father. If you dishonored or damaged my daughter, I could never expect sufficient compensation from you."

Now, most fathers would be tempted by the prospect of marrying off a daughter to such a well-connected warrior. Ailill's kingdom was puny compared to the Brug of Mac Óc. Étaín must have been a terrible beauty, indeed.

"Not to worry," replied the Mac Óc. "I will give you compensation ahead of time."

"So let it be," decided Ailill. Once the terms were set, Ailill was quick to sell his daughter, or so it seemed to the Mac Óc at first.

"Let me hear what you want," said the Mac Óc, sure of a bargain.

"Not too difficult," said Ailill. "You must clear twelve great plains out of the wilderness and woods, making the land fit for grazing herds and for folk to dwell upon, and for sport and racing, and for gatherings and building forts."

"It shall be done," agreed the Mac Óc. He left the house and went straightaway to seek help from the Dagda. The work was done by the next day: twelve plains were cleared from Ailill's lands in a single night. These are the names of nine of those plains: Mag Machae, Mag Lemna, Mag nÍtha, Mag Tochair, Mag nDula, Mag Techt, Mag Lí, Mag Line, Mag Muirthemni.

When the Mac Óc saw that the work was finished, he went back to Ailill, seeking Étaín.

Ailill said, "You will not get her until you have carved twelve rivers flowing to the sea from my springs and bogs and marshes, and drained the lands along the rivers, so that the waters may bring fruits of the sea to all the peoples and kindreds."

Óengus hastened again to the Dagda, lamenting the situation. That very night, the Dagda carved twelve rivers to the sea, where none had been before. These are the names of ten of those rivers: Findi, Modornn, Slenae, Nas, Amnas, Oichén, Or, Bandai, Samuir, Lóchae. When the work was done, the Mac Óc returned to speak to Ailill and to claim Étaín.

The king said, "You shall not get her unless you buy her, for I will get no profit by the girl after you have taken her."

"What do you want this time?" asked the Mac Óc.

"I want the weight of the girl in gold and silver, all for me. Everything you have given so far was for the sake of her kin and her tribe."

"Done," said the Mac Óc.

Étaín stood on the floor of Ailill's hall. They weighed her. Óengus handed over the exact same weight in shining gold and in silver. It would not be surprising if Ailill had put a foot on the scales, for the girl was slight and he was greedy. Mac Óc must have got the treasure from some hoard of the Dagda, for where else would he find so many gleaming torcs and bracelets, sparkling rings and sword-guards, sword-grips, bowls, and other precious ornaments?

Ailill gained wealth and the Mac Óc took Étaín home with him.

What did they talk about, the young woman and the young warrior? She had not witnessed the Mac Óc's challenges and feats (which were really the Dagda's feats). She was not there when they haggled over her bride-price. When they weighed her, she was silent, so far as the poets tell. Who knows whether, before that moment in the chariot, leaving her childhood home, anyone told her that the Mac Óc had sought her hand not for himself, but on behalf of another, older, more cunning man.

Why did Midir not seek the girl himself? Perhaps he was too cautious. Or perhaps he considered his fosterling's childhood triumphs on the playing field and in Elcmar's hall as a promising sign of his abilities. Maybe it was a test.

The travelers reached the Brug and, quick as a blink, Étaín and Midir slept together that very night.

Óengus went to his lonely bed.

The next day, Midir received a cloak suitable to his status and the chariot promised by Óengus as compensation for his wounding. Midir was finally satisfied with his foster son. In fact, he was so pleased that he and Étaín stayed another year at the Brug with Óengus.

That is what the old books say. They do not reveal whether Étaín and Midir spent every night together, whether they were happy and in love, whether they discussed their future, or indeed, discussed anything at all. In the books, there is nary a word from, or about, Étaín during that twelve months.

When the year was over, Midir decided it was time to return to his own territory of Brí Léith.

Likely he did not ask Étaín's preference. She may have been keen to see the lands of her new husband—if, that is, they were legally wed. A rich man could have as many women as he could afford to feed and house, by contract or by mutual agreement, and the occasional slave as well. Sometimes all the women belonging to one man were friendly together, but sometimes they fought bitterly, beating or torturing each other, or worse. The law-keepers imposed penalties for this friction, but when has fear of a fine ever prevented a jealous woman from doing damage?

The Mac Óc spoke to Midir on the day before they departed the Brug. "Keep guard over the woman riding with you, because a fierce and jealous wife awaits you at home—a woman who has the same knowledge, guile, and power as the rest of her people, the Túatha Dé," warned Óengus. "I have given my oath and my guarantee to Étaín that I will protect her from them. You know too well that Fúamnach, your chief wife, is descended from Beothach Mac Iardanél. She is crafty and canny and well-trained in the lore and powers of the Túatha Dé. Remember, she was fostered by Bresal the druid before she married you."

Fúamnach and her dreadful magic were among the things they forgot to tell Étaín, although she might have caught some gossip at Óengus's hall. Still, she was not raised to consider her own happiness. Girls were the property of their fathers until traded, sold, or contracted, after which they belonged to their husbands or masters. A woman always had a man to protect her and speak for her in the company of other men, according to the laws. He kept her safe, or was supposed to.

The story refuses to tell whether Étaín was grateful for the Mac Óc's promise of protection or, indeed, whether they bade each other farewell before she climbed into Midir's chariot for the journey westward, whether she faced bravely forward or gazed mournfully behind her.

Now, that region of Brí Léith belonged to Midir in legendary times. Many hundreds of years after this tale took place, though, Saint Pátraic came along and built a church at Ard Acha near the *síd* of Brí Léith. And when this tale was first written, kings of the tribe of Uí Néill ruled the region. Just so you know.

When they arrived at Midir's hall, his wife welcomed him and gave him a thorough report. She had cared for his property and his people while he was away watching Óengus's boy-troop play bloody hurley, and having his eye healed, and awaiting a first look at his new woman, thanks to the Mac Óc's efforts. Then he spent another year enjoying Étaín at the Brug. Only when he hankered for home did he bring his new woman to meet his wife.

Midir had not made one good decision since he helped Mac Óc win his inheritance.

"Come along, Midir," commanded Fúamnach, "so that you may survey your hall and your lands and possessions, and the king's daughter may see your territory and royal seat." Midir walked about with Fúamnach to review his holdings. She presented his possessions and treasures to him. And to Étaín. Midir then brought Étaín to join Fúamnach at whatever women get up to during the day. What else would one do with a new woman, but hand her over to one's wife? Óengus's words must have slipped his mind. That would be odd though, since Midir had a reputation for being shrewd and sharp.

Fúamnach led Étaín to the house where the women slept and made her sit in a chair that stood in the middle of it. Yet she hissed to Étaín, "You have taken the seat of a worthy woman." Without warning, Fúamnach brandished a wand made of purple rowan. She struck Étaín with it, and the girl dissolved into a puddle on the floor.

In those times, you see, rowan was the wood for magical wands and flails. That or hawthorn.

Dissolving her rival was a desperate move on Fúamnach's part. By law, a wife could beat and kick and scratch her husband's other women, but only so long as she left no lasting mark of harm. If her victim was scarred or began to limp, the perpetrator could have been brought before the law. But a puddle was not evidence. It was absence.

Fúamnach fled to her foster father, Bresal the Druid.

Midir looked in the door of the women's house and found it empty except for the puddle by the chair, so he left. He may have searched for his two wives at first, calling their names, becoming more and more distressed and angry. At some point he must have recalled the Mac Óc's warning.

Midir was without a woman after that.

Meanwhile, the heat of the hearth fire and the warmth of the air in Fúamnach's house, mixing with the life-force of the earth, transformed the puddle of water on the floor into a tiny worm. The worm hatched into a scarlet fly the size of a man's head—the handsomest man in the land. The beating of her wings was sweeter than the music of pipes and harps and horns. Her eyes shone like precious stones on dark nights. Her delicious perfume kept hunger and thirst from anyone who drew near her. The dew off her wings healed the illness and pain of anyone who felt the sprinkle.

The fly attended and accompanied Midir as he wandered his domain. Just listening to her or watching her could encourage whole troops and assemblies. Midir realized that the fly was Étaín. He took no other woman while she stayed with him, for the sight of her sustained him. He fell asleep to her melody. When someone unfriendly approached, she would awaken him.

Faithful insect. Or desperate woman.

After some time, Fúamnach came to meet with Midir. Three of the most formidable of the Túatha Dé came along as her legal protectors, namely, Lug Samildánach the Many-Skilled, grandson of Dían Cecht; Sun-faced Ogma, Ogma the Sage, a brother of the Dagda; and the Dagda himself. It might seem peculiar that the Dagda would protect a woman who had attacked Étaín, given that he had helped the Mac Óc win her, but the Túatha Dé were a closely woven tribe. Or maybe the scribe who wrote this tale mixed up his guarantors. All of Fúamnach's protectors were god-like heroes with adventures of their own, but in this tale they came to assist their kinswoman, the spell-caster Fúamnach.

Midir raged at her. He told her that she would not have escaped alive, but for power of the three guarantors that accompanied her.

Fúamnach said, "I do not rue what I have done. I would rather do better for myself than for anyone else. What is more," she vowed, "wherever I may be in Ériu, as long as I live, I will make Étaín suffer, no matter what shape she takes." Fúamnach had brought terrible glamours and spells from Bresal Etarlám the druid, sufficient to banish Étaín and keep her from Midir. She had already discovered the secret of the scarlet fly that so delighted Midir, for he had not shown interest in a single woman so long as he gazed upon the fly. He took no pleasure in music or drinking or eating when he could not see the fly or hear her wings making delicate music.

So Fúamnach was twice replaced: first by a golden-haired girl and then by a scarlet fly. She conjured a great gale that blew Étaín out of Brí Léith and into the air.

For seven years the fly could not find a roof or treetop or mound or hill on which she could rest, but only the rocks in the sea and stormy whitecaps. She tumbled through the air for seven years to the day until she happened to alight upon the chest of the Mac Óc who was standing atop the mound at the Brug. She clung to him.

There the Mac Óc sang to her:

Welcome,
Wandering woeful Étaín
Blasted by Fúamnach's gale.
You found neither bliss nor peace
In repose at Midir's side.
I myself, meanwhile,
Was mustering many troops,
Hacking my way through the wild,
Seeking treasures worth Ailill's girl.
A labor in vain, it was,

For it brought your wretched ruin.
Yet welcome.

The Mac Óc opened his cloak for the girl-turned-scarlet fly and tucked her inside. He carried her into his house and into his sun-chamber, which was bright with windows for passing in and out. He laid a fine scarlet coverlet over her. Mac Óc transported the sunny bower everywhere he went. He slept by it every night, at her side, comforting her, so that she grew cheerful and calm. The bower was filled with sweet and exotic-smelling herbs, and the fly flourished on the flowering of those rich rare blooms.

Fúamnach heard about the care and respect given Étaín by the Mac Óc. Dead smart, that one. She devised a proposition for Midir and brought it to him.

"Summon your fosterling here so that I may make peace between you, and I shall search for Étaín." Easy to guess why fosterer and fosterling were at odds.

The Mac Óc came to Midir's house to treat with him.

Meanwhile Fúamnach crept out, circled around, and entered the Brug. She raised the same blustery wind to drive Étaín out of the sun-chamber and hurled her into the same crushing flight around Ériu for another seven years.

When the Mac Óc came to reconcile with Midir, Fúamnach could not be found.

Midir's face was dark when he said, "The woman lied. If she finds out that Étaín is with you, she will try to harm her."

"Likely so," said Mac Óc. "Étaín has been in the Brug at my house for some time, in the same shape she had when she was blown away from you. Your chief wife may be after her."

The Mac Óc went home to find the crystal sun-bower empty. He quickly spotted Fúamnach's track and followed her to Óenach Bodbgnaí, at the house of Bresal Eterlám the druid.

The Mac Óc attacked. He struck off Fúamnach's head and brought it back with him to the Brug of Boand. As for the druid, he disappeared from this story. That may have been the Mac Óc's doing, too.

Other poets have other opinions. They say that it was Manannán Mac Lir who murdered Midir and Fúamnach together at Brí Léith. There are verses about it:

> Wretched Fúamnach was Midir's wife.
> Sigmall, a hill of sacred trees.
> At Brí Léith—it was the perfect story—
> They were burned by Manannán.

It is not a perfect story, though. Manannán Mac Lir was ruler of the Irish Sea, king of the Isle of Promise, husband of the delicious Fand, lover of many women, owner of the Cloak of Forgetfulness and the Bottomless Cranebag of Wealth. Why would he wish harm to Midir and his mad wife? That poem must have wandered in from another story. Besides, many adventures still lay ahead of Midir and Óengus the Mac Óc.

As for Étaín, the gale drove her on, in sickness and misery, until finally she blew into a great hall in Ulaid and landed on its roof-pole. Everyone inside was contentedly drinking. The poor, wrecked insect tumbled into a golden cup in the hand of the wife of King Étar the Victorious of Inber Cichmaine. That place was near the Bóinn, or maybe it was a place of the same name farther north, in the province ruled by Conchobar Mac Nessa— surely you know of Conchobar, king of the Ulaid? He commanded the men of Ulaid against Queen Medb and her ruffian troops when she came to steal the Brown Bull of Cúailnge.

It does not matter, because Étar's queen swallowed the fly in her drink.

She became pregnant.

She brought forth a daughter who was given the name Étaín daughter of Étar.

One thousand and twelve years had passed from the birth of the first Étaín, daughter of Ailill, until her second birth as daughter of Étar and his thirsty wife.

Étaín was raised at Inber Cichmaine in Étar's hall. Fifty other chieftains' daughters were reared with her, eating and sleeping with her, and attending her at all times.

One day all the girls were bathing and splashing in the river, when they saw a horseman approaching across the plain. He rode a prancing brown steed, broad shouldered and curly of mane and tail. The horseman wore a green mantle folded about him with a red embroidered tunic beneath. A gold brooch pinned the cloak from shoulder to shoulder. He slung a silver shield rimmed in gold over his shoulder by a strap of gold-bossed silver. He held a five-pointed spear with golden bands running from its haft to its socket. Golden hair fell upon the man's brow, and a twisted band of gold held it from his face.

He paused to watch the girls. They were smitten with him. Then he chanted a poem:

Étaín is here today
At the síd of Bé Find west of Ailbe,
Dawdling with little lads
On the bank of Inber Cichmaine.

She once healed the eye of the king
At the well of Loch Dá Licc.
It was she, downed in a drink
From the cup of Étar's wife.

For her, a king will chase
the birds of Tethbae
and drown his two horses
in Loch Dá Airbreach's waters.

Many battles will surge
Over Eochaid of Mide because of you, girl.
Destruction will come to the síd-mounds
And a war against thousands.

It is she who returned to the land,
It she that seeks the king,
It is she once called Bé Find.
Soon she shall be our Étaín.

When he finished chanting his verses, he rode off. They did not know whence he came or where he went.

Étaín remained still. No flick of her eyes betrayed a memory of the astonishing bard on horseback, yet the mysterious poem proposed both a past and a future with him. It warned that her mute beauty would summon its own storms of destruction. Perhaps she then whispered a forgotten name to herself, tasting it on her lips.

We shall leave her with her secrets for now.

Around that time, Eochaid Airem gained the kingship of
Ériu. Thus it is always written: a man *gained* the kingship.
It means that he waged war, took captives, and razed houses
built on good land along with the creatures that dwelt upon
it and crops that grew there. He bullied the leaders of weaker,
poorer kingdoms and tribes into alliances. He graciously
offered protection and support, which helped him quell fractious chieftains and persuade them to follow him into battle.
They paid him with lodging, feasting, and warriors.

The king of Ériu was the greatest fighter, bully, and
sweet-talker of all, for he commanded the four provincial
over-kings, who likewise commanded all the tribal kings of
the island. When Eochaid took the kingship, the provincial
kings were:

Conchobar mac Nessa of the Ulaid. You know of him
and what kind of king he was, lazing in bed, playing *fidchell*
all day, and lingering in his tent during battle as he plotted
his next move.

Mes Gegra, who took part in the battle over Mac Dathó's
pig, was king of Laigen.

Tigernach Tédbannach shared the kingship of Laigen.
Later, the Ulaid made a hard ball from the meat of his brain.

Cú Roí was the uncanny king of Mumu. He once
pounded Cú Chulainn into the earth and dropped *caca*
on his head.

Finally, Ailill mac Mata Muirisci and Medb were king
and queen of Connacht. A competent bard could tell tales
without stopping for an entire year about that royal couple,
and it would hardly begin to explain them.

These were the main forts of High-King Eochaid
Airem: Dún Frémaind in Mide and Dún Frémaind in
Tethbae, which was near Brug na Bóinne, and Temair of

the Kings, and the fort at the *síd* of Brí Léith, Midir's hall. The fort in Tethbae was Eochaid's favorite residence.

Eochaid proclaimed the Feast of Temair to the people of Ériu just one year after taking the kingship. All his warriors and farmers and herders would gather, bringing their families and servants, at the place where kings of Ériu were made and dues laid. Eochaid would set and collect the rents and tributes he was owed for the next five years.

Uisnech may have been the center of the island, but Temair was its most sacred place. If a man overcame all other kings, he ruled as king of Temair. But the kingship came with conditions. The king was bound by enigmatic prohibitions, *gessa*, which he could not violate: The king of Temair could not linger in bed after the sun rose. He could not break his journey on Wednesday in Mag mBreg or travel over Mag Cuilinn after sunset. He could never strike his horses in Fán Cummair, enter north Tethbae on a Tuesday, or travel sunwise around the fort at Temair.

He was also required to find a queen before he held his inaugural royal feast.

Everyone answered Eochaid's summons, but they all refused to gather at the Feast of Temair to consecrate him as king until he had a queen.

Question? Why should a king require a queen in order to rule?

Answer: Every ruler needs a lady to bear his sons, sit by him in his hall, order his table and house and fields, and comfort him when he returns from battle. Long ago, they say, the king of Temair's true mate was the many-named goddess who protected his kingdom. In the darkness of ancient days, all of Ériu attended the rituals by which the new king consummated his union with his territory. The Sovereignty of Ériu would only yield herself to a man worthy of her, in expectation that his just and generous dominion would bring peace and full harvests to her lands. If, during his rule, mares gave birth to handsome colts, heifers produced calves and plentiful milk, and mortal women brought healthy babies into the world, the king was worthy. If the king turned bad, though—if he treated his people unfairly, was too avid for battle and slaughter, violated his *gessa*, or rendered bad judgments—to be sure, then the earth and its creatures became barren and war convulsed the kingdom until Sovereignty found a better mate.

If a man could not find himself a wife, he could not rule a kingdom.

Eochaid sent messengers to every province, seeking the most beautiful maiden in Ériu. He would only take a woman untouched by any other man. They found such a maiden at Inber Cichmaine. She was young Étaín, daughter of King Étar. Eochaid accepted her, for she was his equal in beauty and figure and family, in reputation and youthfulness and nobility.

Eochaid Airem's father was Find Mac Findloga, who had three sons with his queen and wife. Eochaid Féidlech, the eldest, was Temair's king before Eochaid Airem. Eochaid Féidlech had many children. Four of his daughters married Conchobar Mac Nessa, all at once. Three of his sons rebelled against their father. After Eochaid Féidlech, the kingship passed to his brother.

Ailill Ángubae, the other brother, fell in love with Étaín.

He wanted her at the Feast of Temair as she was wedded to Eochaid Airem. He yearned for her even after she slept with Eochaid on their wedding night. Ailill gazed at her constantly, which was an obvious sign of love. He chastised himself for his obsession, but it did not help because his desire was stronger than his good intentions. He was sick with love but he told no one, not even the object of his passion, for fear of dishonoring himself. And presumably, fear of dishonoring Étaín too, although the poets did not mention it.

King Eochaid was alarmed at his brother's decline. He brought his healer, Fachtna, to examine Ailill as the man dwindled to the point of death. The healer told Ailill, "You have one of the two mortal pains that a healer cannot cure: the pain of love or the pain of jealousy."

Ailill did not admit to anything.

When Eochaid set out on his circuit of Ériu to collect his dues, as was expected of the suitably married king of Temair, he left the dying Aillil at his hall, Dún Frémaind in Tethbae. Étaín remained behind with Ailill so that, as mistress of the household, she might carry out the necessary rituals for her brother by marriage. It was her duty to conduct the funeral and burial, making sure his grave was dug properly, himself keened, and ordering all his cattle to be slaughtered.

Étaín came every day to visit the house where Ailill lay in his sickbed. He seemed healthier whenever she appeared. He stared at her. Étaín noticed it.

One day when they were alone in the house together, Étaín asked Ailill what had caused his affliction.

And that is the very first time in this tale that the fair Étaín said a word. It is possible that Étaín chattered with other women or sang songs to her husband, or even recited entire sagas in Eochaid's hall, but this tale does not know about that. She had not yet spoken to Midir or Mac Óc in our hearing, although she made sweet music with her insect wings. Perhaps it was because Ailill was so weak that she could ask him the question.

"What caused your illness?"

"Love of you," Ailill said.

"A shame that you did not tell me before," she responded. "You would have been cured long before, if I had known."

"I could still be cured if you want," said Ailill.

"I want it, surely," she said.

Were they speaking the same language? Étaín had spent her life—her lives—hovering over men who stared and longed for her. And Ailill? The extra brother.

After that, she went every day to tend Ailill. She washed his face and hair. She brought him news and musicians to entertain him. She accompanied him to meals where she carved his food into tiny pieces so that it went down easily. She poured water over his hands and rubbed them dry.

After three times nine days, with Eochaid still away, Ailill was almost well. He dared to ask Étaín, "When will I get the one thing that I still lack in order to complete my healing?"

We know what that one thing was. Étaín faced a desperate choice: she could heal her husband's brother by lying with him or she could let him waste away while preserving her honor.

"Tomorrow I will satisfy your demand," she decided, "but the affront must not occur in the lord's own house. Meet me on the hill behind the fort."

Did she ever dream of Midir? Did she recall the arresting horseman who caught her bathing and sang to her at Inber Cichmaine? Did she remember her refuge upon the Mac Óc's comforting breast?

That night, Ailill looked forward to his tryst with Étaín, but he was weak and could not help falling asleep. He did not wake until mid-morning the next day.

Étaín kept her midnight tryst with Ailill. At least, he looked exactly like Ailill. He complained of his affliction and said everything that Ailill would say.

The next morning, Ailill awoke from his feverish sleep. When Étaín appeared, he greeted her glumly.

She asked, "Why are you melancholy?"

"I arranged to tryst with you, but I was not there to meet you. Sleep overwhelmed me, and I did not wake until just now." He sagged. "It seems clear that I am not yet cured."

Étaín's eyes must have widened while her mind fluttered its feathers.

"Not so," she told him. "One day follows another."

The following night, Ailill kept watch. He positioned himself next to the crackling hearth-fire and kept a jug of water nearby to dash his eyes.

At the appointed time for their tryst on the hill behind the fort, Étaín spotted the man who looked exactly like Ailill. She rushed back to the house and found Ailill lamenting his loneliness. Three times Étaín dashed up the hill above the fort and three times Ailill remained behind. The man-like-Ailill met her all three times.

"I did not come to tryst with you," she finally challenged the stranger. "Why have you come to meet me? I agreed to tryst, but not to do wrong or harm, only to heal a royal heir of his misplaced passion."

Not-Ailill looked her over from head to toes. "You would do better to meet with me," he said, "for when you were Étaín Echraide, daughter of another Ailill, I was your husband. I paid your enormous brideprice—causing great plains to be levelled and the rivers of Ériu to be dug, and rendering your body's weight in silver and gold so that I might have you." That tongue was silver indeed.

Étaín cocked her head and asked, "What is your name?"

"Easy to tell. Midir of Brí Léith."

"What drove us apart?"

"The sorcery of Fúamnach, my other wife at the time, and the spells of Bresal Etarlám."

When she did not reply, Midir asked, "Will you come away with me?"

Étaín was no longer the naïve lass she had been when Óengus bought her for his foster father. She assessed her suitor's claims. "I shall not come with you. I would never trade the high king of Ériu for a man whose people and kin are unknown to me."

"It was I who made Ailill fall in love with you," Midir pointed out, "I caused his body and blood to waste away. I controlled his lust so that your reputation would not be ruined."

Imagine his face as he said it. Étaín eyed him but said nothing.

He assessed. "If Eochaid allowed it, would you come away with me to my land?"

It was the right query for a woman who stuck by the rules. If Eochaid dismissed her with words of divorce or traded her for something he desired more, Étaín would be free to conclude a contract with someone else. The laws offered plenty of valid reasons for a man to divorce his wife and even a few for women to shed their husbands. Still, even if Eochaid released her from their bond, would she remember the man who had long ago sent his foster son to win her from her forgotten father?

"That is agreeable," she decided. She left without another word and returned to the sick house.

"I am glad you are back," Ailill greeted her. "Not only am I healed now, but there has been no damage to your honor."

"That's good," agreed Étaín.

Soon after, King Eochaid finally arrived home from his circuit of Ériu. He rejoiced that his brother was alive. He offered Étaín great thanks for attending Ailill while he was away.

The ancient Étaín lacked speech and purpose. The recreated Étaín listened and observed before she chose and spoke. She had the wit to detect the impostor. She emerged honorably from a perilous situation, no matter what went on atop the hill behind the king's hall. Yet the voice of Midir of Brí Léith, of unknown descent and kindred, whispered in her ear. *Cétmuinter*, he had called her: "You were my wife."

Midir had spent a thousand lonely years regretting his careless treatment of his bride. Again and again he had failed her. She had good reason to mistrust him and his Otherworldly wiles.

So this time, he plotted an honest courtship of Étaín. Well, almost honest.

In a splendid summery season, Eochaid Airem, king of Temair, rose up and climbed the ramparts of his fort that he might survey Mag mBreg beyond the walls. The fields brimmed with blooms of every color and shade.

If only he had known that the plain was one of seven—or was it twelve?—cleared ten centuries ago by the Dagda, at the Mac Óc's request, so that Midir might win Étaín. Eochaid did not know, though, as he contemplated his dominion, believing his own strength and virtue was responsible for its fertility and the kingdom's prosperity.

As Eochaid glanced about him, he beheld a mysterious young warrior standing near him. The man wore a scarlet tunic, and his golden hair spilled to his shoulders. He had glittering eyes of grey-blue. He carried a five-pronged spear in one hand and, in the other, a shield with knobs of gold on it.

Eochaid did not recall a stranger at Temair the previous night. It was too early for the fort to open its gates to travelers.

The warrior approached Eochaid, who said, "Welcome to a young warrior whom we do not recognize."

"That is why I have come," said the warrior.

"But we do not know you."

"I knew you of old," said the visitor. A small smile lit his beautiful face.

"What is your name?" Eochaid asked.

"Not a well-known one, these days," the warrior admitted. The smile remained. "I am Midir of Brí Léith."

"Why have you come to me?" Eochaid inquired.

"To play a game of *fidchell* with you," said Midir.

Eochaid mused, "I am skilled at *fidchell*." He liked to win.

"Let us find out."

Now *fidchell* is a game of devious strategy. Its players were like kings sending their fighters into battle, one warrior at a time. Old men sat at the board fingering their pieces and reminisced about hard-won victories. Young champions played it while they oiled their swords and awaited real combat. Men and women faced each other over the board, pretending it was a game.

Eochaid remembered, "But the queen is sleeping in the house where I keep my board and pieces."

"I have here a board that is just as fine," said Midir.

It was true. The board was of silver, each corner winking with a precious stone. Its gaming pieces were gold, contained in a small bag of bronze mail.

Midir set out the pieces on the board. "You'll play?"

"I do not play unless we wager," the king said.

"For what stakes then?" asked Midir.

Eochaid shrugged. "All the same to me."

Midir said, "If you should defeat me, I shall render fifty dark grey horses, with blood-dark dappled heads, pointy-eared and strong-chested, nostrils flaring, slim-legged, high-mettled, splendid, superior, swift, steady, and easily bridled with their fifty red-enameled reins—by the third hour tomorrow."

Eochaid promised the same.

They played and Midir was defeated. He left Temair, taking his *fidchell* set with him.

Eochaid rose the next morning and went out on the ramparts of Temair as the sun rose. He saw his *fidchell* opponent approaching along the high bank. The king had no idea where the man had gone or whence he came. Still, when he looked beyond the ramparts, Eochaid saw fifty dark horses with red-enameled bridles on the green below.

"That's proper payment," said Eochaid.

"What is promised is due," said Midir, smiling again. "Shall we play *fidchell*?"

"All right, but there must be a wager," said the king.

Midir proposed with no hesitation, "I shall wager fifty three-year-old boars, their coats curly, dappled, light grey beneath and dark grey above, with horses' hooves, and a black-thorn cooking vat that will hold them all." Before Eochaid could speak, Midir went on, "Also, fifty gold-hilted swords, along with fifty red-eared white heifers with red-eared white calves wearing bronze hobbles. What's more: fifty grey rams, all of them redheaded, three-headed, and three-horned. Fifty blades with ivory hilts. Fifty decorated cloaks. Each of them will be delivered on a different day."

Eochaid's foster father came to him. He asked where the king had got his new wealth.

"Indeed, there's a story there," said Eochaid.

"Is there," nodded his fosterer. "Well, you had best be vigilant, for the man who has come to you has terrible powers. Offer difficult terms, my boy."

Eochaid's opponent awaited him. The king imposed his famous demands: the clearing of stones across Mide, the laying of fresh rushes on Tethbae, the construction of a causeway over the bog of Móin Lámraige, and raising a new forest over the kingdom of Breifne.

A poet once sang these verses about it:

> *These are the four conditions*
> *That Eochaid Airem laid down*
> *Upon the gathering throngs*
> *Armed with spears and swords:*
>
> *A causeway over Móin Lámraige,*
> *Trees across Breifne—easily found—*
> *The wilds of Mide made bare of stones,*
> *Rushes strewn across Tethbae's grounds.*

Those were the conditions and cumbers laid upon Midir, should he lose the game.

"You demand too much," he said solemnly.

"Not at all," insisted Eochaid.

"Then I demand a promise from you. If I lose, permit neither woman nor man in your power to go outside the house until sunrise tomorrow."

"It shall be done," Eochaid agreed. No one ever went into the bog anyway.

Nonetheless, after he won their game and Midir left to fulfill his debt, Eochaid sent his steward to oversee the undertaking of the causeway. The steward crept to the bog, where it seemed that all the men in the world had gathered after sunset. They made a mound of their cloaks and Midir climbed that mound to watch. Whole trees with their trunks and roots were lugged in for the base of the causeway. Midir stood in the middle, conducting the troops on all sides. It seemed as if every man alive was making a racket. After that, they hauled clay and gravel and rocks into the bog.

They say that until that night, the men of Ériu used to harness their oxen around the forehead, but the steward watched the *síd* folk harnessing the beasts at the shoulders. Eochaid was the first mortal man in Ériu to yoke oxen by the neck and shoulders, which is why he was called Eochaid Airem, the Ploughman.

And these were the words on the lips of the marvelous troop as they labored on the causeway:

Put here, put there!
Famous yoked beasts
In the hours after sunset,
'Tis a burdensome demand.
Who shall profit, who shall lose,
From the causeway over Móin Lamraige.

(There is another version of that same verse sung by Midir's men. It is written in the Book of Druim Snechta. To tell the truth, though, it is much the same as this one with a few fancier words added.)

A better causeway would never have existed anywhere in the world if no one had watched them building it. Someone did, though, so the laborers left hidden defects.

The steward reported to Eochaid on the great undertaking that he had witnessed. He declared that no power on the face of the earth could surpass it.

They were still talking when they saw Midir coming along. That morning, his bearing was battle-ready, his face grim. Eochaid rose and gave him a wary welcome.

"For that we have come," said Midir. "It is hostile and unreasonable to have laid such hardships and burdens upon me, and then to violate our agreement. I would have wrought something else, something bigger and better for you, but now my mind is afire with rage."

"I shall not return anger for anger, so let your mind be calm," said Eochaid.

Midir crossed his arms, his eyes hard. "Accepted. A game of *fidchell*, then?"

"What stake?" asked Eochaid.

"Whatever the winner desires," Midir said.

That day, Midir triumphed. He claimed Eochaid's pledge.

"You have won my stake," the king admitted.

"If I wished, I could have done so long ago," said Midir.

"What do you want from me?" asked the king.

"To embrace and kiss Étaín," said Midir.

Eochaid fell silent. Then he said, "A month from today you will be given it."

Eochaid did not know that, one year before Midir first appeared to play *fidchell* with him, the handsome stranger was already wooing Étaín, although he had not won her. Midir called her Bé Find, his Shining Lady, and he sang to her:

O Bé Find, come away with me
To a lovely harmonious land
Where everyone's hair is primrose gold,
Their snow-white skin soft to the hand.

That place has no Mine or Yours.
Teeth white, their brows like night,
A delight to the eye are those noble forces,
And their cheeks are foxglove pink.

Gillyflower-colored, each neck so frail.
How delightful the blue of blackbird's eggs!
Still, however fine the view of Mag Fáil,
It seems desolate after Mag Már.

Though you savor the ale of Inis Fáil,
The ale of Tír Már is far stronger.
More marvelous is that land than all,
Where youth lingers so much longer.

Gentle streams cross the meadows—
Your choice of mead or wine.
A distinguished people without flaws,
Conception without sin or blame.

We see you and the world you're in
But none of you sees us.

The gloom of Adam's mortal sin
Cloaks our hidden numbers.

O, woman, if you come among my proud kin,
A circlet of gold will crown your head.
Honeyed wine, ale, fresh milk to drink,
We will sip there together, Bé Find.

It was a much gentler invitation than the one sung to Connlae by the nameless *timpán*-player. The latter mourned the death of all mortals, but Midir described a life better even than life as Eochaid's queen.

"I shall go with you," said Étaín, "if you get my husband's legal permission. If you cannot get it, I shall not go."

Étaín was still a prize won, lost, or sold by men, but at least she set the terms of the bargain this time.

That is why Midir had approached Eochaid in the first place, and why he lost the first two *fidchell* matches, and why he insisted that no one from Temair should watch when his men cleared the land. When Eochaid's steward peeked, it gave Midir additional cause to quarrel with Eochaid. For Étaín, he took these on near-impossible burdens and crafted an intricate plot leading to an unnamed stake in the last round. Midir set a meeting to collect his kiss in one month.

I told you he was a wily bargainer. He knew the minds of men and the precepts of law better than he knew his own mother, whose name is lost to us.

Still, Eochaid was almost as wily.

Eochaid mustered the best warriors and the elite of the *fian* bands at Temair, positioned in concentric rings around the fort, outside and inside the ramparts. The king and queen remained in the very middle of the hall. The gates were locked, for they knew that the man of mysterious powers would come on the appointed day. Étaín was dispensing drink to the lords that night, for it was her special skill and duty as queen. She may have been cool as water from the well or she may have quivered and glanced at the door as she poured. You never knew with her.

They were roaring and gabbing when they saw Midir inside the king's house. He was always handsome, to be sure, but that night he was even more magnificent. The troops were dumbstruck.

The king welcomed him.

"I have come for this," Midir said. "Let what was pledged to me be handed over. What was promised is due. What I myself pledged was given to you already."

That was legal talk.

Eochaid said, "I hadn't thought about it much until now."

"Étaín herself promised me that she would leave you."

Étaín blushed. At last, a sign of love from her!

"Do not be ashamed, Étaín," Midir said to her softly, "Your promise was not unwomanly. I have been courting you for a year, offering the greatest treasures and wealth in Ériu. I did not try to carry you off without Eochaid's permission. I would not win you by my powers alone."

He could easily have taken her, just as he could have won the first *fidchell* game. But would Étaín have whispered sweetly to him after that? Her esteem had become his heart's goal.

"I told you," said she, "that I would not give myself to you until Eochaid agreed to sell me. That is my decision: You may take me if Eochaid sells me."

I will certainly not bargain you away," declared Eochaid, "but he can put his arms around you here in this house, as was promised."

"Done," said Midir. He seized his spear in his left hand and caught the woman tightly in his right arm. Then together they rose up into the air and disappeared through the smokehole of the roof.

Somewhere, in the back of her mind, Étaín must have remembered how to fly. All those years of buzzing over Midir's head prepared her to unfurl new white wings and sail through the skies, safe from furious wives and mortal kings who spied on their opponents at *fidchell*.

Midir may have maneuvered Eochaid like one of his silver game pieces in order to win back Étaín, but Eochaid never stipulated against shifting shape or flying away while the couple enjoyed their embrace. Midir knew the rules of play and the ways of bending time better than anyone.

Let us hope Midir also got his kiss.

The warriors surrounding the king leapt up at this outrage as they watched two swans circling high above Temair. The pair headed for Síd ar Femin.

Eochaid gathered the elite fighting men of Ériu and followed the pair to Síd ar Femin (also called Síd Ban Find after Étaín.) This was the counsel of the fighters of Ériu: Dig up every *síd* in Ériu until the woman was returned.

The troops dug first at Síd Ban Find, but someone came out and told them that the woman was not there. "The man who came to you is king of all the *síde* of Ériu. He is in his royal fort with the woman. Go on until you reach it."

The army went northward. For a year and three months they dug up *síd*-mounds. Yet the holes they dug one day were always filled with earth again on the next day. If there was one thing Étaín excelled at, it was staying out of the way. As for Midir, he loved a challenging game more than anything except Étaín.

Two white ravens flew out of the *síd* and two dogs came out, named Scleth and Samair.

The men of Temair went southward again to Síd Ban Find. They start digging into the mound. Someone came out and demanded, "Why are you here, Eochaid? We did not seize your wife. We did not injure you. You must not dare say anything harmful to a king."

"I will not go away," said Eochaid, "until you tell me how I can get my wife back." He should have known that a *síd*-creature cannot be trusted to tell mortal truths.

"Take blind whelps and blind cats and let them go at it. That is what you must do each day."

Eochaid left then, taking the animals with him, and did as he was advised.

They were digging at the *síd* of Brí Léith when they spotted Midir approaching.

"Why are you here?" Midir asked Eochaid. "You played unfairly and imposed burdensome demands on me. You sold your wife to me. Do not trouble me again."

"She will not stay with you."

"Then she shall not," Midir shrugged. "Go home. Your wife will come to you at the third hour tomorrow. The one thing is as true as the other," he promised. "Now stop persecuting me, if you are satisfied with this arrangement."

Eochaid accepted.

Midir secured his promise and went his arrogant way.

At the third hour of the next day, Eochaid and his men watched a band of fifty women coming toward them. All of the women had the exact same form and appearance as Étaín. The troops fell silent.

A grey hag led the woman troop. She rasped to Eochaid, "Choose your wife according to the arrangement, or tell one of these women to remain with you. Then the rest shall depart your house at once."

Eochaid turned to the men of Ériu. "What would you do, given the dilemma before you?"

"We have no idea what to do," they admitted.

"Well, I do," said Eochaid. "My wife is the best at pouring drink in all Ériu. I shall recognize her pouring."

Twenty-five women were put on one side of the house and twenty-five on the other side. A vat of ale was brought to the middle of floor. A woman came from one side to pour drinks for the men, then a woman came from the other side, and so on in turns, but Étaín did not seem to be among them. It came down to the last two women. One of them poured first.

Eochaid declared, "This is Étaín, although she is not herself today."

All the men conferred together. "It is Étaín, but not her usual way of pouring," they agreed.

The other women departed.

The men of Ériu were delighted at Eochaid's accomplishment and pleased, too, with the job done by the oxen that helped plough the mounds, and the rescue of the king's woman from the men of the *síd*.

❦

One fine day not long after, Eochaid rose. He and his queen were conversing on the grounds of the fort when they saw Midir coming.

"Greetings," said Midir.

"Greetings," said Eochaid.

"You acted unfairly toward me," Midir told him yet again, "by imposing terrible obligations on me, bringing troops against me, and everything else you demanded. There is nothing that you have not demanded from me."

"I did not sell my wife to you," said Eochaid.

"Is your mind settled with me?"

"Unless you propose another pledge, I will not be bothered about it."

"And have you peace of mind?" asked Midir.

"I do," said Eochaid.

"As do I," Midir said.

Imagine his grin as he went on.

"Your wife was pregnant when I took her from you, and she bore a girl. That girl is right in front of you. Your former wife is with me. You have lost her again."

And then he disappeared. He did not say what became of all the other Étaíns, whether they dissolved like smoke, or followed the hag to pour drink for other men, or married kings.

Eochaid did not dare attack the *síd* mounds again because he had sworn that he was satisfied. He was distraught that his wife had left him and that he had slept with his own daughter. The latter became pregnant and bore him a daughter.

"Gods above! Truly, I will not look at the daughter of my daughter," said Eochaid. Two men from his retinue took the babe away, planning to throw her in an animal pen. They came to the house of Findlám, the herdsman of Temair, which was on Slíab Fúait in the middle of the wilderness. No one was in the house. The two soldiers ate what they found there and left the girl with a bitch and her pups in a pen. Then they went away.

The herdsman and his wife came back to the house and found a small, fair child in the pen. They were amazed. They reared her without knowing where she was from. She grew into a fine young woman. She was, after all, the daughter of a king and queen. She was as handy as anyone. There was nothing that she could not embroider. Thus was she raised by Findlám and his wife until one day, King Étarscelae's men caught sight of her beauty and informed him. She was seized and brought to Étarscelae to become his wife. She became the mother of the renowned Conaire Mac Étarscélae.

You may know his tale, but I shall not tell it here.

So many Étaíns. The poets often mix them up because it is hard to tell one from the other, as Eochaid discovered. One storyteller claims that a woman named Étaín married Étarscélae and had a daughter by him whom they named Étaín, and that she was the girl baby thrown in an animal pit. That baby, too, was rescued and raised by herders. One day, that young Étaín saw a bird on the skylight of their house. It descended, took off its bird-suit, and became her uninvited lover. He made her pregnant, but she passed the child off as the son of Étarscélae. As the story goes, "Lovely are all until compared with Étaín, dear are all until compared with Étaín." No man could keep her, though, except a son of the Túatha Dé.

As for Eochaid Airem, he was in Fremaind at Tethbae after he lost Étaín—actually he lost two Étaíns—feeling dejected. Sigmall Cael Ua Midir, the son of Midir's daughter Ogniad, eventually came to burn down Dun Fremaind around Eochaid. Supposedly, Sigmall took Eochaid's head to Síd Nendta in revenge on his grandfather's behalf.

But it may not be true, because Sigmall and Fúamnach, first wife of Midir, were allegedly killed by Manannán Mac Lir at Brí Léith during the rule of the Túatha Dé Danann—unless it was Midir and Fúamnach killed there, or someone else entirely.

What I would like to know is, what did Óengus get up to that whole time?

"*Timpán* in hand, she made music for me every night."

THE THIRD TALE

Aislinge Óenguso—The Dream of Óengus

THE MAC ÓC HAD MANY adventures. If we sat telling them until Doomsday, we would not have told them all. Óengus Mac ind Óc and Ogma were at the Battle of Mag Tuired when the thunderous Túatha Dé defeated the water-borne Fomoire. Later in life, the Mac Óc was foster father to Diarmaid Ua Duimhne, the *fian* warrior who stole dainty Gráinne from none other than the mighty Finn Mac Chumhaill.

Some sages insist that Óengus played a god of love, like an Irish Cupid who plucked at a harp as he gave away kisses. The Scots say that he dwelt in Tír na nÓg and rode a fancy trick horse. But none of that is true.

Óengus was famous for his hospitality at Brug na Bóinne. His hall was built for feasting. It was 700 feet across and had four doors, pillars of wood from faraway Cyprus, and a roof of woven birds' feathers. There was room for 150 men in it and a cauldron that could boil 160 wild boars at once (it is always good to have extra for a feast). The best thing about the Mac Óc's hall, though, is that the drinking there never stopped. It had plenty of space for a family, too. Óengus Mac ind Óc was clever to have bargained such a house away from Elcmar.

Everyone agrees, however, that Óengus Mac ind Óc's greatest adventure took place when he fell in love with a bird-girl.

The start of this story will sound familiar. The poets often echoed and hinted at stories that took place before and after. This tale combines too many sly references to list. Try counting them as we go along.

One night, Óengus awoke to a strange sight: a woman approached his bedside.

Not that he lacked women. He was the Dagda's offspring, after all. Óengus's devotion to Étaín, wife of his foster father, was well known, though never explained.

Still, when this woman appeared to him, he thought: She is the loveliest one in Ériu.

Óengus reached for her arm, hoping to tug her into his bed, but she sprang away from him. He could not see where she had gone.

All the clues pointed to a visitor from the *síd*. There are ways of recognizing those folk, in addition to their sudden appearances. They are ravishingly gorgeous, with bright clothing and plenty of gold on them, riding or driving first-rate horses. They favor green cloaks. Sometimes they simply shine. They can disappear, shift shape, and fly through the air. They are present one moment and gone the next. Óengus had to know that his visitor came from the Otherworld because he came from there, too—although the story doesn't say.

He lay awake until the next morning, considering the phantom and feeling feverish. His mind was not well. Óengus was not, as they say, *slán*. It means healthy in body and mind or healthily without love, the worst of men's afflictions. For instance, Étaín's brother-in-law, Ailill, was not *slán* when she missed her trysts with him. *Slán* also means recovery from childbearing. The Boand was *slán* again by the time her husband, Elcmar, came home from his mission to the north, although she had grown pregnant and borne a son to the Dagda while Elcmar was out.

Óengus was not *slán*. That day, nothing passed his lips. He lay in bed until night descended.

Here she came again with a *timpán* in hand, a little harp sweet as could be, and made music for him until he fell asleep. Again, he lay in bed until the next day without eating. For a full year, the maiden visited him in this way, so that he fell hopelessly sick with love. He never said a word to anyone. He was desperately ill, but no one knew why.

All warriors, from Connlae to Cú Chulainn, hate admitting any sort of weakness.

The healers of Ériu gathered to help him, but at the end of the day they could not discover the cause of his ailment. They sent for King Conchobar's own healer, Fergne, who hurried to Óengus. (Or else his name was Fíngen, but this story calls him Fergne.)

Fergne could diagnose an illness by glancing at a man's face. By observing the smoke from a chimney, he could reckon the number of people ailing inside a house.

He took Óengus aside. "Well, your situation is unlucky," said Fergne. "You are sick with love from afar."

"You have found out my illness," said Óengus.

"You let yourself sink into a shameful state and you have not dared to tell anyone about it," said Fergne.

"True," said Óengus. "A beautiful woman came to me, her figure more luscious than any in Ériu, her appearance the most exquisite. *Timpán* in hand, she made music for me every night."

"No worries," Fergne told him. "Love has overwhelmed you. Let us send messengers to Boand, your mother, so that she may come and advise you."

Things were serious if they were calling for his mother.

Boand was summoned and so she came.

"I have been trying to heal the lad of an ailment that has flattened him," said Fergne. He explained the case to Boand. "His mother should tend to him. Search all of Ériu to find a girl that looks like the one your son saw."

They searched for a year, but they did not find a girl like her.

They summoned Fergne again.

"Her like could not be found," said Boand.

Fergne suggested, "Send for the Dagda to come and confer with his son."

The tales do not say whether Boand was still close to Óengus's father, though the attraction between them had once been fierce. Perhaps Boand and the Dagda had put their tryst behind them. Yet, as the Túatha Dé remained inexplicably beautiful, Eithne the Boand was still as appealing as the day when the Dagda first saw her.

The Dagda was summoned and so he came. "Why was I sent for?" he growled.

"To counsel your son," said Boand. "It is proper that you talk to him. It is pitiful that he is dwindling away. He is sick with love for a disappearing girl, and no help can be found."

"Why do you need my advice?" the Dagda asked. "My wisdom is no greater than yours."

"Surely it is greater," said Fergne, "for you are the king of the *síd*-mounds of Ériu. Send for Bodb, king of the *síd*-mounds of the province of Mumu, for his wisdom is famous throughout all Ériu."

The Dagda knew that, for Bodb was also his son. Bodb was one of the kings who led the Túatha Dé off the surface of Ériu and into the *síde*. (Advice: Do not try to sort out the timelines of the Otherworld, you will only go mad as a *geilt*, grow feathers, and take to the trees. The time of tales cannot be reconciled with mortal chronology.)

Bodb was found. He received the messengers. "Welcome, men of the Dagda."

"That is why we have come."

"What is the news?"

"Just this: Óengus, son of the Dagda, has been sick with love for two years."

Bodb raised his eyebrows. "How did that happen?"

"He saw a girl in his sleep. We do not know where in Ériu the girl could be. The Dagda enjoins you to search all Ériu for a maiden of her form and appearance."

Woman: absent. Shape: shatteringly lovely. Form: *timpán* in hand. Behavior: Disappears at dawn.

"We will search for her," said Bodb, "I will keep at it for a year until I find her."

They returned at the end of the year to Bodb's house at Síd ar Femen.

"I searched all over Ériu for an entire year until I finally found the girl at Loch Bél Dracon at Crotta Clíach," announced Bodb.

Messengers returned to the Dagda. He eagerly welcomed them home. "What did you find out?" he asked.

"Good tidings. The girl you described has been found. Bodb asks that Óengus return with us, the messengers, to see whether he recognizes the girl."

Óengus was taken in a chariot to Síd ar Femen. King Bodb prepared a great feast to welcome him. They spent three days and nights celebrating.

It was polite in those days to feast first and negotiate after.

Finally, Bodb suggested, "Let us go and find out whether you recognize the girl that you saw in your dreams. But remember: Even if you recognize her, I cannot give her to you. We can only look."

They traveled then to the lake, where they discovered three fifties of nubile women. The elusive maiden was among them. She stood taller than the rest. A silver chain linked each pair of girls, but Óengus's woman wore a silver collar about her neck and her chain—unattached to any other— was of burnished gold.

Bodb said, "Do you recognize the woman?"

"I recognize her," nodded Óengus.

"I can do nothing more for you," said Bodb.

"Never mind," said Óengus, "she is surely the one I saw. I cannot take her away now, though. Who is she, Bodb?"

"I know her, certainly," mused Bodb. "She is Cáer Ibormeith, daughter of Ethal Anbúail from Síd Úamain in the province of the Connachta."

Connacht. One of the four provinces of ancient Ériu. Connacht's territory stretched from Loch Rí in the middle of the island all the way to the rocky coastlands of the northwest. It was the kingdom of Medb and Ailill in those times. You might know their names. If you do not, you soon shall.

Óengus and his men went home. Bodb came along to visit the Dagda and Boand at the Brug of Mac ind Óc.

They shared what they had learned and explained that the girl was the same in shape and form as the one that Óengus saw. They revealed her name, her father's name, and her grandfather's name.

"Unfortunate," said the Dagda, "that we cannot get her."

Bodb suggested, "It would not be a bad thing, Dagda, to consult Ailill and Medb, for the girl is in their province."

The Dagda went to Connacht with three scores of chariots. They were welcomed by the king and queen. They spent a full week feasting and drinking.

The royal couple of Crúachu must have realized that their guest was the god-man over all others and leader of the Túatha Dé. Why, one might ask, would that mighty divinity, thousands of years old, seek the advice of mere mortal heroes from history?

It is all part of a tale that leads to another tale, so wait for it.

The king asked the Dagda, "What brought you here?"

"There is a girl in your territory," said the Dagda. "My son has fallen in love with her and it has laid him low. I came to find out whether you would give her to the boy."

"Whose is she?" asked Ailill.

"She is Ethal Anbúail's girl."

"We do not have the power," said Ailill and Medb. "If we did, we would give her to Óengus."

The Dagda considered and suggested, "You should summon Ethal."

Ailill's steward went forth and announced to King Ethal, "You are summoned to a consultation with Ailill and Medb."

"I will not go," said Ethal, cunning father. "I will not give my daughter to the Dagda's son."

The steward brought back bad news. "He cannot be made to come and, what's more, he knows why he has been called."

"Not a problem," said Ailill, who often spoke dryly. "He will come, all right, and the heads of his warriors along with him."

After that, Ailill's men and the Dagda's troops set out to attack Ethal Anbúail's *síd*-mound, just like the old days, when *síd* fought *síd*. They razed the mound and brought three score heads as well as the king, whom they kept captive in Crúachu.

Ailill said to Ethal Anbúail, "Give your daughter to the son of the Dagda."

"I cannot," said Ethal. "Her power is greater than mine."

Shame and more shame to the father. Still, it made the woman seem even more precious in the eyes of the Túatha Dé.

"What great power does she have?" asked Ailill.

"Not hard to tell. She takes the shape of a bird every other year. In the other years, she takes human shape."

"What year will she be in the shape of a bird?" asked Ailill nonchalantly.

"I will not betray her," said her father.

"I will have your head unless you tell us," said Ailill.

"I will tell you," said Ethal, "since you are so determined to find her anyway. When the next Samain is near, she will be in bird form on Loch Bél Dracon, and wondrous birds will be there with her, and three fifties of swans surrounding her. I shall prepare all."

"It will not be necessary," scoffed the Dagda, "I know the shapeshifting nature that you yourself have cast upon her."

They all swore an alliance then, that is, Ailill and Ethal and the Dagda. Then they turned Ethal loose.

The Dagda bade them farewell. He went home and told the exciting news to his son. "Go next Samain to Loch Bél Dracon and call her from the lake to you."

The Mac Óc did exactly that. The following Samain, he traveled to Loch Bél Dracon. He found 150 white birds on the lake with silver chains about them and golden curls on their heads.

Óengus stood in human shape at the shore. He called, "Come talk to me, Cáer."

"Who calls me?" Cáer asked.

"Óengus calls you." The one you stalked by night for a whole year. The one wrecked with longing by your seductive *timpán*-playing. The man that you invited with one eye and resisted with the other.

Cáer said, "I will come to you if you vow that I may return to the lake."

"I vow it," said he.

She went into his arms. They coupled in the form of two swans, circling the lake three times.

That is how he avoided breaking his vow—she came out of the water for him, but he cast them into swan-shape for a blissful three laps so that, just as she had demanded, he brought her back to swandom in the lake.

He had learned from a master how to talk his way around a promise.

Then they rose up in the form of two white birds and flew all the way to the Brug of the Mac Óc. As they glided over his home, they sang wistful melodies that put all the people below to sleep for three days and nights.

Cáer stayed with Óengus after that.

Some poets say that this story's whole purpose is to explain why Mac Óc came to help Ailill and Medb in their later (mis) adventures. In thanks for their assistance in finding Cáer, he brought three thousand men to the army of Medb and Ailill when they went on the great cattle raid, the *Táin Bó Cúailnge*. Whether he brought mortal men or *fir síde*, I could not say. The tale stands on its own, though, without considering the future of that greedy couple. Like Connlae, Óengus was lured into loving a musical phantom woman. But Connlae's adventure led to the sinless Land of Promise. In this tale, Óengus mates with his bride and brings her home.

You might wonder why the son of the Dagda and Boand, who won Étaín on behalf of his foster father, could not find Cáer Ibormeith without the help of the *síd* and human rulers.

Hard to say. Sometimes the tales betrayed the unearthly nature of the Túatha Dé and sometimes the stories kept it secret for the audience to discover. It depends on the story's purpose, its teller, the teller's place, and the season. Also, it is amusing to watch heroes struggle once in a while.

It also depends upon the woman at the heart of the tale. Cáer Ibormeith was no Étaín, who meekly obeyed men's orders. Cáer was a powerful bird-girl who ignored the wishes of her father and her king. She chose Óengus when he was dreaming in bed and again by the waters at Loch Bel Dragon.

"From the highest branches, she caught sight of a fire in a clearing of the forest below."

THE FOURTH TALE

Tochmarc Becfhola—The Courtship of Becfola

IT IS A TRICKY TASK to tell a venerable story. There is always someone in the audience who knows the story as well as you do and waits to correct you. Other listeners grow weary of the devices and clichés used to describe famous characters, or they grow bored with the formal dialogue of lovers. Still others skip the poems tucked into the narrative like the seasoning on meat. They demand more love, more sex, more blood, more jokes. They propose different endings for the tale. A good storyteller welcomes these interventions. Nowadays, however, a reader greets every tale in private on the pages of a printed book or digital screen. It is hard to rouse a silent story from its slumber and persuade it to perform.

But a story should be pliant enough to suit everyone, don't you think? This tale is heedless of genres and cycles. It is a literary shape-shifter. It begins with another bold beauty who brazenly courts a great king from medieval history, named Diarmait son of Áed Sláine, a descendant of Níall of the Nine Hostages. He ruled the territory of Brega and, it seems, assumed the high-kingship at Temair more than seven centuries after King Eochaid Airem lived and lost Étaín. Someone jotted the news of Diarmait's death in the *Annals of*

Ulster, kept by monks at Ard Macha. 665: *Mortalitas magna. Diarmait m. Aedo Slane . . . don bhuidhe Chonaill,* "A great die-off. Diarmait mac Áeda Sláine . . . from Conaill's Plague."

Many stories about Diarmait came to life during and after his thirty-year reign. Diarmait's foster son Crimthann Mac Áeda was also real and died, according to the same annals, in 633. In this tale, Crimthann was sent to Diarmait from the men of Laigen (Leinster) as a hostage, in order to guarantee peace between kingdoms. Kings often took hostages from the losing side after a war or from enemies who wanted a peace treaty. The presence of the hostage among hostile warriors in a king's fort was supposed to curb the subject king's aggression, for if the lesser king violated the terms of the treaty, the hostage would be executed. Sometimes a hostage was welcomed and treated well in a foreign court, and might even be accepted as a foster son of his official captor, as in this story. Other hostages did not fare so well, though. If the peace fell apart and the fighting began again, their bodies could be sent home in bits or found in a bog. That too was reality. And as the tales of the Mac Óc teach us, the relationships of fosterage were ever fraught with tensions and legal obligations. Fortunately, in this story, Diarmait and his foster son Crimthann were of the same mind about important matters, including Christian virtues and the highly tempting lady, Becfola.

Some scholars think this is a king-tale, because Diarmait was a real king, but it takes the title of a courtship tale, *tochmarc.* Despite its mooring in the annals, this tale of courtship does not march in a solidly historical direction. Instead, it rushes from one peculiar turn of events to the next, leading readers out of a *tochmarc* in the direction of a tragedy of passions, which could easily have led to an *aided.* The story then becomes an *échtrae* or adventure story, and next a battle story, until finally a saint invades the tale and calms everyone down. You might also note that the tale contains more than one courtship.

What's more, while the story of Óengus's love-dream delicately echoed other stories, this tale is a purposeful patchwork of literary bits and pieces. It could be that a lousy bard stole its episodes from other tales and blithely crammed them together to make *The Courtship of Becfola*. Still, the tale has its own logic, and that logic belongs to the protagonist, Becfola. She is at once wooer and wooed. She is from the *síd* but falls witlessly in love with an unknown warrior. After Becfola guides her ornate chariot into the tale, you might expect her to be a famous metaphor for sovereignty, but she is a bad queen, untrustworthy wife, and terrible foster mother.

Wait till you see. Becfola does not meet anyone's expectations, nor does she meet the end you might expect. Every awful decision made by Becfola turns out to be the right one. Is she a heroine, a wanton, a pagan, or a *ban síde*? I'll tell you what: She is funny.

Discuss it afterward, will you.

Diarmait son of Áed Sláine was king of Temair. Crimthann son of Áed was his foster son and also his hostage, taken into custody as a pledge of peace from the men of Laigen. One day Diarmait and his foster son Crimthann went to Áth Truim, between the rivers Bóinn and Cluain Dabhail. The pair brought along only one servant to attend them, instead of the usual retinue.

Diarmait and Crimthann beheld a woman in a chariot crossing the ford from the west.

You might remark some clues to this interesting situation.

First, it is true that travelers in Ireland commonly met at fords in a river, because that was the only way to cross the rivers. Bridges were rare. *Áth* means a ford. *Truim* is elderflowers. The ford was ten miles away, as the crow flies, from Diarmait's home at Temair.

Second, close by this particular ford stood a church that had been founded by Saint Pátraic himself in the fifth century, and which he graciously gave to Saint Lommán. It stood there in Diarmait's day. Later on, Norman invaders built a tidy castle at the ford and changed the name of the place to Trim.

Third, the woman was coming from the west. The *síd* was always to the west. Connlae and his fancy woman sailed westward in a crystal boat at the end of his Adventure.

What is more, as the woman came closer, Diarmait and Crimthann saw that she wore sandals with round toes of white bronze, decorated with precious stones. Her bright-bleached tunic was embroidered with red gold and over it she draped a crimson cloak. A brooch of wrought gold, shimmering with a rainbow scatter of stones, pinned the cloak over her chest. Bands of refined gold circled her neck and bound her brow. Two dark grey horses pulled her chariot, bridled in gold, and the yoke that joined them glinted with silvery animal designs.

King Diarmait asked the proper question. "Whence have you come, woman?"

"From not far away," said she.

"Why have you come?" asked Diarmait.

"To seek seed wheat. I have fertile land but no suitable seed." What kind of look did she cast him? It was effective.

"If you like the seedlings in this land," said Diarmait, probably smirking, "I could do your sowing for you."

The strange lady replied, "I shall not refuse, if you give me the price that I deserve."

In other tales, a bold woman like this one might cause suspicion, all dressed up and driving alone with gold weighing her down, and a cloak dyed the color of royalty. That may be what Diarmait was thinking, with his puns about sowing seeds. Her appearance and her unexpected arrival suggested that the old goddess of sovereignty had come to Diarmait, as the tale expects us to notice.

Diarmait ruled Temair, although sometimes in company of his brother or another king. He could easily have spared a few cattle and some nice jewelry for her bride-gift, especially given that the lady might be symbolically granting him exclusive possession of Temair. But Diarmait said, "I shall give you this small brooch."

The lady was nonplussed. "It is acceptable," she nodded.

She never told him her name or her parentage, let alone her motive. No one asked, maybe because they believed her to be a supernatural metaphor. Crimthann said not a word about Diarmait's manners.

Diarmait brought the woman to Temair, to the hall of the king of Ériu.

"Where did the woman come from?" everyone asked.

"She did not say," answered Diarmait.

"What did you give as a bride-gift?" they all inquired.

"My little pin," said Diarmait.

"The price is truly small." Everyone laughed at the pun. In the old language that was: *Is becc ind fhola*. Unclear whether they laughed, too, at the woman's low worth.

"That will be her name then," said the king's druid. "Bec-fhola. Little Value."

You might think that a man who made jokes about seeds and sex could have come up with a better nickname than that, one that did not remind everyone of his strange bargain.

As it turns out, Becfola was silent but watchful. After the wedding, her thoughts swiftly turned to Diarmait's young foster son, Crimthann Mac Áeda. Sovereignty is fickle. So, it seems, was Becfola. She could have approached Crimthann when they first met at Áth Truim, before she promised herself to Diarmait, but she waited until she established herself at Temair.

For days, weeks, months, Becfola solicited Crimthann. She yearned for him. Finally she persuaded the lad to meet her at Cluain Dá Chaillech—the Church of the Two Veiled Sisters, which sat a little south of Temair—at mid-morning (that is, at the third hour of the monastic liturgy). The tryst was set for Sunday. Crimthann would elope with her.

It seems like poor planning. The third hour arrives in full daylight. Also, at that time in Ireland, no one was supposed to work on the Christian Sabbath. Plenty of good Christians were coming and going to church. The Sisters of Cluain Dá Chaillech might have noticed lovers canoodling in the back garden.

Crimthann revealed his secret plan to those closest to him, the retinue he brought from home to serve him in his hostageship. His outraged people counseled him against abducting the wife of the high-king of Ériu, his foster father and captor. Crimthann rethought his response to Becfola.

Oblivious to Crimthann's moral dilemma, Becfola rose up from Diarmait's bed early on Sunday morning, ready for adventure.

"What are you doing, wife?" Diarmait asked groggily.

"I have a problem," she sighed. "Some of my possessions are still at the nuns' house in Cluain Dá Chaillech. The servants left them behind and ran off."

"What possessions are these?" he grumbled.

Becfola ticked them off on her fingers. "Seven embroidered shifts, seven pins of gold, and three golden circlets. It would be a pity if they went astray."

"Do not go on Sunday," growled Diarmait. "It is not right to travel on Sunday."

She ignored him. "Someone must go with me."

"It will not be one of my men," snapped Diarmait.

By my count, Becfola had already committed three sins in a row: adulterous lust in her heart, lying, and intent to travel on a Sunday. When she left the king's house, the majestic scion of a proud line of kings remained abed until time for church.

Becfola brought her handmaid on the journey southward from Temair toward Dubthar Laigen to the south, where they got lost and wandered about until nightfall. In the rustling darkness, they were ambushed by wolves. The beasts quickly gobbled up the handmaid. Becfola escaped by scuttling up a tree where, from the highest branches, she caught sight of a fire in a clearing of the forest below.

How long did it take for the wolves to finish their gruesome meal and slink away to look for the next? That is how long she waited before climbing down and approaching the fire.

She found a young warrior roasting a pig at the fire. He wore a brightly bordered silken tunic, stitched all over with circles of gold and silver. On his head was a cap, or was it a helmet, of gold and silver and crystal. Golden bangles caught his tresses, which fell all the way to his shoulders; that is, two spheres of gold bound his plaits at the neck, each bauble as big as a man's fist. His gold-hilted sword was tucked in his belt and two five-pronged spears were laid on the belly-leather of his shield, which was adorned with a boss of white bronze. A multicolored cloak was on the ground beside him. His two arms were covered to the elbows with ornaments of gold and silver.

Never mind Crimthann, Becfola had found someone as brilliantly clothed as herself.

She went to sit by the warrior at the fireside. He noticed her but did not give any sign of it as he finished cooking the pig. He made a meal of it. Then he washed his hands and left the place.

Without a word, Becfola followed him to the lakeshore, where a boat of bronze floated in the water. A bronze chain secured the boat to the shore, and another chain stretched all the way to an island in the middle of the lake. The warrior grabbed the chain and hauled the boat to shore.

Becfola hopped in the boat before him. When they reached the island, they left the boat at a boathouse built of clay near the landing place.

Bronze boat, crystal boat, such mysterious vessels sailed through these tales.

Becfola entered the house first. The interior was breathtaking, its sturdy walls encircled by numerous niches with couches that became comfortable beds.

He sat. She sat beside him.

He reached out a hand and a platter of food appeared before them. They each ate and drank their fill, although neither became intoxicated.

There were alone in the house. They did not speak to each other when he climbed into bed. She crawled under his cloak and lay between him and the wall. He did not speak, touch, or turn to her during the night.

As taciturn as Crimthann, then.

Early in the morning, they heard a call from the jetty.

"Come out, Flann, the men are coming!"

He rose up then and armed himself, and went outside. Becfola followed and watched out the doorway. She saw three men at the jetty, exactly like Flann in looks, age, and physique. Then she observed four more men at the jetty who stood ready with shields.

Flann and his three look-alikes charged the four attackers. The two quartets smote each other until everyone was red with enemy blood. Then all the wounded men staggered away.

Flann was the only one left standing. He returned to the house.

"A victory befitting your bravery," Becfola praised him. "That was a heroic combat."

"It would be better if I fought against genuine enemies," he said grimly.

"Who were the attackers?" she asked. They had surely seemed like enemies.

"They are the sons of my father's brothers," said he. "The other three, who fought by my side, are my brothers."

"What were you fighting for?" she asked.

"This island," he said.

It must have been precious territory. It was often thus with families that split and argued over an inheritance. Also, the house was very nice, the food was good, and the magic strong.

Becfola asked him, "What is the name of the island?"

"The Island of Fedach Mac in Daill."

"And what is your name?"

"Flann, grandson of Fedach," he answered. "The grandsons of Flann are fighting against each other for inheritance of the island. This is a very good island. It can supply meals for a hundred, both food and drink, every day, without labor or laborers. Yet if only two people occupy the island, it offers only enough provisions for them."

Becfola demanded, "Why should I not stay on the island with you?"

"Because our union would be disastrous for you," he said. "If you stayed with me and abandoned your husband, the king of Ériu, you would have to accompany me into battle and, likely, exile."

Midir never made this kind of fuss. Étaín never demanded his partnership. For them and for other mismatched couples, their future was something to be fashioned together.

Becfola was confident of her heart's will. "Why will you not sleep with me?"

"I cannot now," he said. "But truly, if I win this island and if we survive, I shall come for you and make you my wife forever. You must go now, though."

Becfola stalled. "I am sorry to leave my maid behind."

He said patiently, "You will find her alive at the base of the same tree where you hid. The warriors of the island protected her. They will escort you now."

That was so.

❧

Becfola returned home to find Diarmait only just rising on the very same Sunday of her early departure, although she had passed a night and a day on the island.

"I find it amazing, wife," said Diarmait, "that you did not actually travel on Sunday anyway after I forbade it."

"I would not dare to disobey your words," she said modestly, as though she had not gone anywhere at all.

From that moment on, Becfola used to sing a poem:

I spent a night in the woods
In the house of the Island of Macc in Daill.
Though I went with a man, I did not sin.
We parted too quickly for me to fall.

The island of Fedach Macc in Daill
In Laigen, in Dubthar;
Although near the road,
Bearded warriors cannot see it at all.

Everyone found that poem strange.

Exactly one year later, the doorway of King Diarmait's house blew open. Over the threshold staggered Flann, sorely wounded.

To everyone's shock, Becfola addressed the visitor sharply. Perhaps she was snappish because it took Flann so long to fulfill his promise:

I doubt the valorous feats
Of those who fought on Dam Inis,

Was it the same four that beat
The other four on Dam Inis?

Flann replied:

Woman, do not hurl rebuke
At warriors for the fight's outcome;
They were not honorable men who broke,
But men with poison-tipped spears.

She said softly:

I cannot defend myself
Against a man's assault
When it is Flann who was cut
In the fight of the equal eight.

Becfola fell into Flann's wounded arms. Diarmait did not try to prevent her following Flann out of the house. "Let the devilish woman begone," he groused, "for no one knows where she is going nor whence she came."

Everyone was still talking about it when four young clerics arrived at the house.

"Whyever are clerics traveling on Sunday?" Diarmait demanded. He tugged his cloak over his head to cover his eyes so that he would not look upon sinners.

"We travel under the permission of a venerable holy man," announced one cleric. "We do not impose upon you from sheer willfulness. Molaise of Dam Inis bade us come to speak with you. A stalwart of our community was rousing his cows this very morning when he sighted four armed men, their shields held low and ready, advancing along the island of Dam Inis. He watched another foursome confronting the first band. They clashed together. The din of clattering shields could be heard across the whole island. Silence fell after they were all slain except one sorely wounded man who escaped alive. The other seven were taken away and buried by Molaise."

"What's more," the cleric went on, "the warriors left as much gold and silver as two monks could carry—the spoils of everything they wore under their cloaks, about their necks, on their shields and spears and swords, and on their arms and tunics. We offer this news so that you might assess the portion of that gold and silver owed to you as king of this territory."

The monks were obedient taxpayers.

The king was a charitable Christian.

"I shall not take anything," Diarmait declared. "I shall not collect a share of what God has given to Saint Molaise. Let some precious emblem of his church be made from the gift of gold and silver."

So it happened. From that silver and gold the treasures of Molaise were crafted, that is, his shrine, his traveling altar, and his staff.

Becfola disappeared with Flann Úa Fedaig and never came back.

Where did the lovers go? Not to Flann's island, because after he won it from his cousins, Saint Molaise seems to have claimed and renamed it—unless the poets mixed up the several islands named Daim Inis, not to mention about forty different Saint Molaises. There was a Saint Molaise who had a Daim Inis, but that was far north in Loch Erne.

By law, Diarmait could have banished his wife. In other tales, the king might have killed her or her lover on the spot. Diarmait had doctrine on his mind, though. He was more repulsed by Sabbath-breakers than by adulterers, and remained hopeful of Molaise's blessing upon his kingship— or so the biographers of Saint Molaise suggested. Besides, Diarmait was keeping his seed-wheat for a woman who never frolicked on a Sunday.

"No one knows where she is going nor whence she came," was a familiar phrase pronounced by Diarmait. It hinted that Becfola was a heathen *ban síde* like those in the oldest legendary tales, who could not find peace in the newly Christian world. The goddess of sovereignty was useless to a king favored by the Christian God.

Whatever the men in the story thought about Becfola's forward and impious ways, she boldly proposed not one, but three courtships in this tale and came away pleased. That also pleases me.

"Deep was the darkness of that night and great the horror."

THE FIFTH TALE

Echtra Nerai—The Adventure of Nera

NERA WAS NO HERO. HE was not a king, a king's son, or a renowned warrior. He was merely one spear-carrier among many in the household of Connacht royalty, namely, the inimitable Queen Medb and her husband, Ailill Mac Máta. Nera happened to be among the men sheltering at Ráth Crúachan on one eventful Samain eve.

Samain marked the passing of autumn into winter when the sun retreated and nights lengthened. The dark was for talk, drink, sex, sleep, and a good game of *fidchell*. No one wanted to be out on a shivery night, especially not at Samain eve, when the veils between worlds fell away and doors to unseen halls swung wide. One reality spilled into another.

Ráth Crúachan, capital of Connacht, had been a portal to the *síd* long before Ailill and Medb came to rule it. In and around its main mound with the fort on top stretched acres of plains and hills dug with ancient barrows, processional avenues, stone rings, and ritual mounds. For millennia, royal bodies of the Connachta were laid in the earth with chanting and keening, but the dead remained present somehow even after their bones had melted away and their tombs had collapsed. They kept watch over their descendants. The reverent living built their farms and forts nearby, sometimes even atop ancient graves, under the protection of their revered ancestors. On the hill at Crúachu, the rulers of Connacht stood with (and upon) their forbears, gazing for miles over a countryside riddled with places both religious and historical. The man who ruled from Ráth Crúachan was one of the mightiest kings in Ériu, and his wife was a mightier queen.

But on the eve of Samain, no matter who you were, if you were breathing, you gathered your folk and your pets inside, locked your gate, and closed all the doors and windows. Once the portals to the *síd* blew open, a soul caught outside could meet his worst dreams. You might be striding along and suddenly find yourself in an unfamiliar land, with no clue about the way home. Some adventurers could not resist a quick peek at the Otherworld, to their lasting regret.

Nera was not one of them. The night he entered the *síd*, he was too busy to wonder which world contained him. Nera never carried out a proper courtship, although like better-known heroes, he found a woman for himself in the *síd*. His *echtra* began when Ailill and Medb were still content together, before they began arguing about their riches and Medb decided she must rustle some cattle.

Ailill and Medb were in their fort of Ráth Crúachan on the eve of Samain with all their household and retinue. They were just boiling up their meat for supper.

They had hanged two lawbreakers on the previous day. Now, as they lazed around the hearth, Ailill proposed to the assembled, "If anyone would bind a withe hoop around the foot of one of the convicts hanging on the scaffold, he shall have a reward from me of whatever he wishes." A withe is a flexible, slim branch from a willow.

That was a king who knew how to enjoy himself on Samain eve, daring his men to halt their feasting and drinking to play dangerous games in the dark with hanged men.

Deep was the darkness of that night and great the horror. Just so you know, demons always hovered nearby on Samain eve. Always.

One man at a time blustered, caught up his sword, and crept into the night to meet Ailill's challenge, but each warrior quickly scurried back into the house.

Finally Nera said, "I will get that treasure from you. I shall go out."

"You shall have my gold-hilted sword," promised Ailill.

So Nera found a sturdy spear and headed out to survey the hanged men. He brought a withe and bound it around the foot of one of the dead men, but the withe would not form a ring and hold together. He tried three times. Though withes are so pliant that little girls can weave crowns made of them, they resist strong knots.

The convict suggested that, if Nera did not put a proper peg on the withe, he would not be able to secure it around the dead man's ankle, even if he kept at it until the next morning. He must use the right peg. Nera accepted this advice and secured the withe with a proper peg.

You note that the dead man spoke.

Nera's adventure should have been over. He had braved the terror of Samain, fulfilled Ailill's dare, and earned his sword. If only he had dashed back to the house.

The convict shouted praise from the scaffold. "That was manly, Nera!"

"Manly indeed," agreed Nera.

"By the honor of your manliness, take me on your back so that I might get a drink with your help. I have been thirsty all day since I was hanged."

"Come on my back then," said Nera.

A hero would never have agreed to such an imposition. The man dropped onto Nera's back and clasped his neck.

"Where should I carry you?" asked Nera.

"To the nearest house," said the hanged man.

The approached the house. They saw something strange then: a lake of fire surrounded the house.

"There is no drink for us in this house," decided the convict. "In that house, the fire is always properly banked at night. Go to the next nearest house, then."

They went to it. They a saw a normal lake of water around it.

"Don't make for that house," ordered the convict. "There is never a washtub or a bathing tub nor a trough with slops left inside after they go to bed. They empty them all out. Go to another house."

Nera carried him on.

"There's surely a drink for me in this house," said the convict.

Nera dumped him on the ground, and the dead man went into the house. Wash water and bath water remained standing in tubs. The dead convict drank from each of them. A trough full of slops sat on the floor of the house. He drank from that as well. He spat his last mouthful over the faces of the people sleeping in the house, and they all perished of it.

It is never a good idea to leave the wash or bath water standing, or to neglect banking the hearth fire, or to leave slops in the house after bedtime.

Afterward, Nera carried the hanged man back to his torture on the gallows.

Then he returned to Crúachu where he came upon something dreadful.

The fort was burnt to the ground. The heads his of people were hacked off and stacked in a heap.

Nera caught sight of the retreating enemy and tracked them into the cave below Crúachu.

You might know it: it's called Uaimh na gCat or Owneynagat, Cave of the Cats. Not cats like your sweet puss-puss, but cats that grow larger than a house, with fire for eyes and daggers for teeth. The cave looks like just a small dark hole at the base of the hill, but once you crawl inside you are lost in a labyrinth of lightless tunnels forever.

Unless you do as Nera did and follow men of the *síd* on the eve of Samain.

"A man has joined the troop," the last warrior in the enemy band told Nera. He took him for a comrade.

"The troop is heavier," agreed the man next to him. Each man passed along the word, from the last to the leader.

Síd folk walk lightly, you see. They can dance across the grass without bending the tip of a single blade. Only mortals leave footprints.

They reached the *síd* of Crúachu and went inside.

A display of heads was erected for the satisfaction of the king of the *síd*.

A question: How, you might ask, did someone precede the warrior band, gathering the heads strewn around the smoking ruins of Ráth Crúachan, and carrying them back to the *síd*, to pile tidily, before Nera and the band arrived?

Answer: Easy to say. These men were *fir síde*. They are faster and stronger than we are. They can move between worlds without missing a mortal second.

Or else: The one who taught this story to the one who taught it to me forgot that Nera saw the heads heaped over the earth at Ráth Crúachan.

Or else: There were enough heads to make two piles. Never mind why—men of the old days liked to display their trophies.

"What should be done with the man who came with you?" someone demanded.

"Let him come out and speak to me," ordered the king.

Nera approached him.

The king asked, "What brought you into the *síd* with the warriors?"

"I followed the troop," said Nera.

"Go to the house yonder," said the king, "there is an un-married woman there who will welcome you. Tell her that I sent you. And bring a load of firewood here to my house every day."

All was done as ordered. The woman greeted him. "Welcome to you, if you are the one sent by the king."

"I am," Nera confirmed.

That was another wonder, to wander into the *síd* and be given an amiable farmwife. By the king's command, Nera lugged a bundle of firewood to the fort every day. Each time, he saw a blind man leaving the fort ahead of him, carrying a lame man on his back. They went to visit the well near the gate of the fort.

Every day, the blind man asked, "Is it there?"

And every time, the lame man responded, "It is, so let us go from here!"

Later, Nera asked the woman about that. "What do the blind man and the lame man seek at the well?"

"They visit the crown that is in the well," said she, "a golden diadem for the head of the king. It is kept there."

"But why do both of them go?" Nera persisted.

"Easy," said she, "because the king decided that those two were most suitable for checking on the crown. One man was blinded and the other lamed."

So neither could steal the crown. Kings! Ailill sent his men to fool with a corpse. The king of Crúachu's *síd* sent the halt and the sightless to guard his crown. One wonders how they came by their injuries.

"Come here for a bit," said Nera to his woman, "so you can explain something about my adventures."

"What happened to you?" asked the woman.

"Before I came into the *síd*, it seemed to me that Ráth Crúachan was laid waste and that Ailill and Medb, with their entire household, were slaughtered."

"That's certainly not true," said the woman. "It was a phantom host that came to Crúachu. That vision will become true, though, unless you reveal the plot to your friends."

"How might I warn my people?" asked Nera.

"Go back," said she, probably thinking him a simpleton. "They are still sitting around the same cauldron and the meats have not yet been taken off the fire."

Yet it seemed to Nera that he had spent three days and nights in the *síd*.

She went on. "Tell them to be ready on the next Samain, or else come to destroy the *síd* before that—for has been foretold of them: Ailill and Medb shall destroy this *síd* and seize the crown of Brión."

By the by, these were the three treasures in the *síd*: the mantle of Lóegaire Mac Néill to be kept in Ard Macha; the crown of Brión Mac Echach Muigmedóin of Connacht; and the tunic of Dúnlang mac Énnai Niad of the Laigen, which went later to the church at Cill Dara.

And why were they precious? Lóegaire, Bríon, and Dúnlang were famous kings of legend—though they lived after the time of events in this tale—whose many descendants ruled whole provinces. Thus, those who possessed the relics acquired royal powers.

Nera asked, "How do I prove that I have been in the *síd*?"

"Bring the fruits of summer with you," said the resourceful woman.

So he brought with him wild garlic, primrose, and golden fern, all of which bloomed in spring.

The woman also said, "I will soon be pregnant by you and bear you a son. Send news to me when your people are coming to destroy the *síd*, so that I can lead your household and herd out of danger."

And what did Nera do next? Embrace his woman with joy? Snatch her up and take her with him? Nera was never that excited.

Nera went to his people. He found them gathered around the same cauldron, cooking their meat. He told them his story and he took his sword from Ailill in reward for the withe incident.

He waited with his people for a whole year.

That was the very year, to be specific, when Fergus Mac Róich left the Ulaid to go into exile with Ailill and Medb at Crúachan Aí.

That was after Fergus's foster son Noíse was murdered by King Conchobar, which led to the suicide of the young warrior's sweetheart, Deirdriu. There is a sad tale about Noíse and Deirdriu.

And that is why Fergus was with Medb when she embarked on the famous cattle-raid of Cúailnge, instead of at home defending the Ulaid against her armies.

"The time has come, Nera, for your return," Ailill finally announced. "Go and fetch your household and animals out of the *síd* before we destroy it."

Nera trudged back to his wife in the *síd*. She welcomed him. "Go out to the fort," she ordered Nera, "and carry a bundle of firewood with you. For the whole year I have been hauling a load of wood on my back every day in your place. I told the king that you were ill. Oh, and there is your son yonder."

What a treasure of a woman! As stoic as her man.

He went out to the king's fort then, carrying a load of firewood on his back.

"Welcome back from your sickness!" said the king. "By the way, it was improper of the woman to sleep with you without asking our permission."

What had he expected when he sent Nera to her?

"Let your wish be done," said Nera.

"I will not make it any harder for you," said the king. He had already imposed a servile duty on Nera.

Nera came back to the house.

"Tend your cattle today," said the woman. "I gave your son a cow as soon as he was born." Nera went out that day to mind his herd.

While he was napping, the Morrígan stole his son's cow and took it eastward, where she allowed the massive bull Donn Cúailnge to mate with the cow. Afterward, Morrígan returned westward with the cow.

Morrígan—her other name was Badb—was a mischievous shape-shifter when she wasn't at war. She tumbles into Nera's story along with Fergus, not to mention another great hero whom you might recognize.

Cú Chulainn overtook Morrígan in Mag Muirthemne on her return—for it was one of Cú Chulainn's *gessa* (his mysterious prohibitions) for a woman to leave his territory without him knowing. It was *geis* for a bird flock to graze his land unless they left something behind. It was *geis* to let fish swim into his estuaries unless he himself caught them. It was *geis* for foreign warriors to enter his land in the evening unless he confronted them by the next morning; if they should come in daytime, he had to face them that same day. Every marriageable girl and woman among the Ulaid was under his protection until she was handed over to a husband. These are the *gessa* of Cú Chulainn. Some of them, anyway.

Cú Chulainn overtook the Morrígan with her cow and said: "The cow must not be taken!"

He sensed the trouble that would follow, when Queen Medb would plot to steal the marvelous bull that was born to the cow of Nera's son . . . that is yet another, very long story.

Nera came home in the evening with his herd. "My boy's cow has gone missing," he said.

"I do not deserve this poor herding," his woman complained.

The cow came along then.

"How strange! Where did the cow come from?" asked Nera.

"She came back from Cúailnge," said the woman, "after being bulled by the Brown Bull of Cúailnge. Get along now," she said, "lest your warriors bestir themselves. The marauders are prevented from raiding until the next Samain. They will go out on the next Samain eve, for all the *síde* of Ériu always open on Samain."

Nera went home to his people.

"Whence came you?" asked Ailill and Medb, "and where were you since you left us?"

"I was in fair lands," said Nera, "with riches and great wealth, with an abundance of cloaks and food and marvelous treasures." He displayed his summer fruits. Then he broke the bad news: "They will come to destroy you on the eve of next Samain, unless you devise a plan."

"We will attack them before Samain," said Ailill.

The people of Crúachu went on with their lives until the end of the year—although Nera now had two lives really, what with the woman and child and farm in the *síd*.

Finally the day came. "If you have anything in the *síd*, Nera," said Ailill, "fetch it out now."

So, three days before Samain he brought his flocks and his household goods and his wife and child out of the *síd*. The new bull-calf came out of the *síd*, too, that is, the calf of Aingen's cow—Aingen was the name of Nera's son. It gave three bellows. At that very moment, Ailill and Fergus were playing *fidchell*. They heard the bellows of the bull-calf in the plain. Then Fergus said,

> *It does not make me happy, the calf*
> *That bellows in the plain of Crúachu.*
> *Dub Cúaligne's son signals woe,*
> *The young bull beyond Loch Loíg.*

He'll cause calves without cows
In Bairrche, in Cúailnge,
The king will set a long course
For the bellowing bull-calf of Aingen.

There is a brief story about Aingen's calf. The Morrígan, all dressed in hideous red, turned into a scald-crow. She argued furiously with Cú Chulainn in that tale, too, and predicted the greatest of all cattle-raids and also the Cú's own death, all because of that calf. Afterward, the bull calf and the Finnbennach—the White Horned Bull—met on the plain of Crúachu. They battled day and night until finally the calf was beaten. The calf bellowed when he was defeated.

"What made that noise in the distance?" asked Medb of her servant. His name was Buaigle.

"I know it, Old Man Fergus," interrupted Bricriu the Poison-tongued, "that is the song you sang this morning." Did Bricriu mean Fergus was fated to be defeated? Or that he bellowed like a calf from Medb's bed?

Fergus glanced at him sidewise and struck Bricriu's head with his fist. The five *fidchell* pieces he had been holding in his fist drove into Bricriu's head and thereafter caused long-lasting pain to him.

"The calf bellowed to say," Buaigle went on, "that if his father should come to fight Finnbennach, the latter would be beaten from one end of Mag nAí to the other."

Then Medb vowed an oath: "I swear by the gods that my people swear by, I will not lie down, nor sleep on goose down or featherbed, I will not drink buttermilk, I will not care for my body, I will not drink red ale nor white, and I will not eat until those two bulls battle before me."

After all that blustering, the Connachta and the Dark Exiles that accompanied Fergus got around to invading the *síd*. They hauled out everything of worth and then destroyed the place. They found the crown of Brión, one of the three wonders of Ériu.

But Nera returned with his household to the *síd*, and he has not yet come out. He will not come out till the end of the world.

Perhaps the folk of the *síd* survived that attack after all. Ailill's men did not bring home any heads, only treasures. Nera still had his sensible wife and his son and cattle, and Aingen still had his calf. Nera cherished Ailill's sword, which he had won in a trial by withe. I am guessing that he left off carrying firewood to the king and became a soldier of the *síd*. At the very least, he managed to avoid the cattle-raid to come, the one led by Medb that would cause more bloodshed than any other war among the Irish of those days.

"The golden ring lay atop the salmon."

THE SIXTH TALE

Táin Bó Froích—The Cattle-Raid of Fróech

LIKE NERA, FRÓECH COULD COME and go from the *síd*. Although his father was a mortal man from Connacht, his mother was Bé Find—the Fair Woman, the Shining Lady, the Bright One. Bé Find could mean White Cow, too, but to my ear, Bright Lady sounds more respectful.

A Bé Find, in rega lim, sang Midir to Étaín once, as she splashed in the water with her maidens: O Bé Find, will you come with me? Perhaps another of Étaín's incarnations was as Fróech's mother, but there is no tale that says so. Such ladies were elusive. This Bé Find was the sister of another great mother of the *síd*, Boand.

Family in the *síd* had its advantages. Your kinfolk were beautiful, immortal, and wealthy and, what is more, they could wield magic. Mortal parents could be more difficult. Ailill and Medb manipulated their children for their own selfish purposes, as in this tale and the story of the great Cattle-Raid of Cúailnge. The story of that *táin* flows as an underground current through this *táin*, which is more like a romance of Fróech and Findabair. Some poets will tell you that this tale, too, exists merely to explain why Fróech brought his troops to help Medb in the Cattle-Raid.

Although it is also called a *táin*, there is no rustling in this tale until the end. Scholars quarrel about whether it began as a tale told around the fire or was composed by an imaginative monk at his writing table. Still others propose that, in a version lost long ago, Fróech did not court Medb's daughter but sought Medb herself. Fróech died in the great *táin*. Or he died in a raid on the *síd*. Across the waters in Alba—the old name for Scotland—they sang ballads about Fróech's death for five hundred years or more. In the ballads, Medb is a jealous villain who sends a water monster after Fróech. Listen for hints of her vengeful nature in this version of the tale, too. The Ailill in this story is a cruel opposite of the serene ruler in Nera's tale.

We might call this a courtship tale, but it is a trifle melancholy for that, even though it tells of the mutual yearning between a woman and a half-Otherworldly hero. Everyone in this story is double-tongued and calculating, except the keening women of the *síd*. The first part of the story is fleshy with detail. The second part is nothing but bones.

One more thing: I'm fairly certain that this tale, like the tale of Becfhola, is supposed to be funny.

Fróech son of Idath of the Connachta was also the son of Bé Find of the *síd*, and she was sister to Boand.

He was the handsomest warrior among the men of Ériu, but he did not live long.

His mother gave him twelve white red-eared cows from the *síd*. He practiced good husbandry for eight years without taking a wife. Fifty was the number of kings' sons residing in his household, all the same age and all equals in body and beauty.

Findabair, daughter of Ailill and Medb, fell in love with Fróech after hearing stories about him that reached all the way to Crúachu. News of his reputation spread throughout Ériu and Alba. It occurred to him to go and speak with the girl. He discussed this with his people.

"Go to your mother's sister first," they advised, "so she can give you marvelous garments and other gifts from the *síd*."

The tie between a man and his mother's siblings was almost as important as the tie between foster child and foster parent.

Fróech went to Boand, who lived in Mag mBreg. He got fifty blue cloaks, each of them iridescent as a beetle's back, with four corners of dark grey on every cloak, each caught with a red-gold brooch. Fifty tunics of snowy white with interlaced animals stitched in gold upon them. Fifty silver shields with golden rims. A candle fit for a king's house in the hand of every man, and fifty rivets of white bronze upon each candle, and fifty coils of refined gold around each. Carbuncle decorated the spear butts, and the spearheads were made of precious stones. They shone in the night like rays of the sun.

Now you may be asking: Why were warriors carrying decorated candles?

They were not. It is a poetic way of saying spears. Candles are lit with fire, you see, just as the spears of mighty warriors can be inflamed with fierce valor, especially if the warriors come from the *síd*.

They had fifty gold-hilted swords. The fifty men rode dappled grey horses, and each horse wore a gold bridle-bit, a silver-bedecked collar from which tinkled a little golden bell, and a crimson saddlecloth with silver fringe, secured with a pin of gold and silver fashioned with an animal head. Fifty horsewhips of white bronze with little gilt hooks at the tip. Seven greyhounds in silver chains with a golden ball between each pair, and wearing decorated bronze greaves—there is no color that wasn't on them.

What's more, seven horn-blowers with horns of gold and silver, wearing colorful garments, with hair of a gold that only comes from the *síd*, and gleaming cloaks. Three fools capered before them wearing silver-gilded crowns. The three carried shields with engraved designs and spiral ornaments, and with bronze strips along their edges. Three harpists dressed like kings surrounded each fool.

They left for Crúachu.

A watchman at the fort saw them coming into the plain of Crúachu.

"I see a troop approaching the fort," said he. "Since Ailill and Medb took the kingship, there has not come, nor will there come, a troop more noble or splendid. The breeze that wafts from them makes me feel as if I have plunged my head into a vat of wine! One young warrior sports and performs a trick whose equal has never been seen: He casts his spear ahead of him and, before it reaches the ground, seven hounds with silver chains have already caught it."

Then the hosts went out from Crúachu to have a look. They crowded together so eagerly while trying to get out of the fort that sixteen men were crushed to death.

The visitors dismounted at the entrance. They unharnessed their horses and unleashed their dogs. They hunted seven deer to Ráth Crúachan and seven foxes and seven hares and seven wild boars, and the young warriors slew them on the green before the fort. Then their hounds leapt into the river

Bréi and took seven otters. They brought their catch up to the entrance of the royal hall.

The company sat down there. The king sent a messenger to meet them, asking whence they came. They gave their names—their true names—"The men of Fróech mac Idaith." The steward reported to the king and queen.

"Welcome to them," said Ailill and Medb.

"The young warrior is amazing," said Ailill. "Have him come inside the gate."

A quarter of the house was given over to the men. This is what the house looked like:

Seven concentric rings of curtained bed chambers circled the space from the central hearth fire to the round walls of the house. Each ring was divided into seven sleeping chambers—couches draped with curtains for privacy. Bronze metalwork framed every bed chamber. A carved and decorated panel of red yew separated the chambers. Three strips of bronze marked the platform under each chamber.

Seven pillars of copper, stretching from floor to roof, circled the enormous vat filled with drink.

The house was made of pinewood and its roof of wooden shingles. There were sixteen windows in the house, each with a copper shutter, and a copper grating over the skylight.

That was a grand house, to be sure. No other royal house in any story could compete. It was finer than the house of Flann Úa Fedaig on his uncanny island (although, to be fair, that house produced magical meals every day). Much more impressive than the hall of Eochaid Airem, one-time husband of fair Étaín.

At the center of the house, four more copper pillars ornamented in bronze surrounded the couch of Ailill and

Medb. Two borders of gilded silver edged it. A silver panel on one side reached up to the crossbeams.

After circling the hall from one door to the other and having a look, Fróech and his men hung up their weapons and settled down. They were received hospitably.

"Welcome to you," said Ailill and Medb.

"It is what we have come for," said Fróech.

"Then it shall not be a back-and-forth journey," said Medb. She meant that he would find what he sought within her house.

Medb played *fidchell* with Ailill after that. Fróech began playing it with one of the men from his troop.

Fidchell, as you know, is a delightful way to pass the time and take one's ease after a punishing day of riding and hunting. The game offers an opportunity for competition without weapons as well as a chance at seduction, depending, clearly, on the inclination of one's opponent.

Fróech's *fidchell* set was beautiful. The board was of white bronze with corners and edges of gold. A torch of precious stone illuminated the gold and silver pieces upon the board.

"Offer food to the warriors," said Ailill.

"I do not wish to," said Medb. "Instead, I would play *fidchell* with Fróech."

"Fine. Go to him," said Ailill.

She played *fidchell* then with Fróech.

It was just a game.

Meanwhile Fróech's troop roasted the meat they had killed.

"Let your harpers play," said Ailill to Fróech.

"Let them play," agreed Fróech.

The musicians had harp-bags made from otter's hide and Parthian leather decorated with gold and silver. The kid-skin covers over the harps were white as snow with dark grey spots like eyes in the middle. Coverings of linen over the strings were white as swan's plumage. The harps were of gold and silver and white bronze, with snakes and birds and hounds of gold and silver crawling over them. When the strings moved, the creatures twirled among the crowd.

The harpers played then, and so poignant was the melody that twelve men of died of grief-stricken weeping then and there.

Fair and melodious were those three harpists. They were the fair ones of Úaithne, a famous trio composed of three brothers, Goltraiges, Gentraiges, and Súantraiges. Their names meant Grief-music, Laugh-music, and Sleep-music. Boand of the *síd* was their mother. They were named for the music that Úaithne, the Dagda's harper, played while Boand was giving birth. At first, the music was woeful and sorrowful because of her keen pangs. Then, in the midst of delivery, the music was joyous and welcoming because of the mother's delight at delivering two sons. Finally, the song was drowsy and gentle when she brought forth a third son, on account of the strenuousness of the last birth. The third lad was named for the third, somnolent kind of Úaithne's music. When Boand awoke from her sleep, she said, "Receive your three sons, Passionate Úaithne. Forever, sad music, joyful music, and sleepy music will play to the heifers and women that give birth in Medb and Ailill's territory. Men will die from the melodies of merely tuning the harps."

The harpers stopped playing music in the royal house.

"A champion has come," remarked Fergus. He mostly kept out of sight in this tale.

"Share out the roasted game that was brought into the house," commanded Fróech, still at *fidchell* with Medb.

Lóthur, one of Fróech's men, strode into the center of the house. He divided the food among all of them. He carved each portion with his sword, cutting meat on the palm of his hand, but did not even scratch his skin or the flesh. From the time that he took on the job of carver, no scrap of food was ever lost in the cutting.

Meanwhile, Medb and Fróech played *fidchell* for three days and nights by the full light of the precious stones that shone upon the followers of Fróech.

When they finally ceased playing, Fróech addressed Medb. "I have done you a favor," said he. "I did not win your stake at *fidchell*, since it would have caused you a loss of face."

"This has seemed the longest day ever spent in this fort," said Medb.

"It was," agreed Fróech. "It lasted three days and nights."

Then Medb rose up and was ashamed at the warriors going without provisions for three days. She went to tell Ailill.

"It's a terrible thing we have done," said she, "leaving the visiting warriors without food."

"You preferred to play *fidchell*," said Ailill.

"It should not have prevented feeding the troop in the house. It was three days and three nights," said she, "but we did not notice because of the bright illumination of the gems inside."

"Tell them to stop playing games," said Ailill, "until food can be distributed among them."

Food was given them then, and it was all so pleasant that Fróech and his men stayed there feasting for three more days and nights.

After that, Fróech was called into the royal house of council and asked what brought him to Cruachú.

"We wanted to enjoy a visit with you," said he.

"Indeed, our household is happy with your presence," said Ailill. "Your visit will be better if you extend it rather than end it."

"We will stay then," said Fróech, "for another week."

They stayed for a fortnight, hunting every day near the fort. The local people would come to watch them.

Fróech, however, was frustrated that he had not yet spoken privately with the girl Findabair, since it was she that had drawn him to Medb and Ailill's Ráth Crúachan.

One day, at dawn, he rose to wash at the river. That was also the hour when Findabair went with her handmaid to wash. When they met, he took her hand. "Stay and speak with me," he said. "It is for you that we have come."

"I would welcome you before everyone if I could," said the girl, "but I cannot."

"Will you run away with me?" he asked.

"I certainly will not elope," said she. "I am the daughter of a king and queen. You are not so poor that you cannot get me from my people. Then I would gladly go with you, for I have loved you from afar. Here, take this ring," said the girl, "it shall be a sign between us. My father gave it to me," said she, "but I will say that I lost it."

They parted then.

"I fear that our daughter will elope with Fróech," said Ailill.

"That would not be all bad, for he could come with his cattle to help us on the cattle-raid," Medb suggested.

Fróech came into the house of council. "Are you having a private discussion?" he asked.

"There is room for you," said Ailill.

"Will you give me your daughter to wife?" asked Fróech.

Very bold the man was, for better or worse.

"I would give her," said Ailill, "if you rendered the bride-price that we set."

"You will have it," promised Fróech, but he had not yet heard the terms.

"I want three score dark grey horses," said Ailill, "with golden bridle bits on them, and a dozen milch cows, and a drink of milk from each one, and a white red-eared calf with each cow. And you must come with all your men and your musicians to help rustle the cattle of Cúailnge. My daughter will be given to you if she agrees."

"I swear by my shield and my sword and apparel, I would not give that bride-price for Medb herself." Fróech strode out of the house after that. He refused the bride-price, and Findabair refused to elope. It was a quandary.

Ailill and Medb conferred. They had a habit of promising Findabair to any warrior who would help with their cattle-raid. If they finally gave her to any one of them, the rest would be outraged.

Ailill said, "A multitude of kings of Ériu will lay siege around Crúachu if we give our daughter to Fróech. It would be best to start after him and kill him at once before he can cause us harm."

"That is a dreadful plan," said Medb. "It would dishonor us."

"It will not dishonor us," said Ailill, "if arranged properly." Ailill and Medb then entered their royal hall.

"Let us go out," said Ailill to all, "to watch the hounds hunting until midday, when they tire."

After watching the hounds, they all went down to the river to bathe.

"They tell me that you are good in the water," said Ailill to Fróech. "Jump into the pool here so that we may see you swim."

"What sort of pool is it?" Fróech asked.

"We do not know of anything dangerous in it," said Ailill. "It is bathed in frequently."

So Fróech disrobed and went in, leaving his belt on the shore. Ailill meanwhile slid over to examine the clothes. He opened the purse attached to the belt. The ring was in it.

"Come here, Medb," hissed Ailill.

Medb came to him.

"Do you recognize this?" asked Ailill.

"I do," said she.

Ailill heaved it into the river below.

Luckily, Fróech saw him. Fróech also saw the salmon that shot out of the water above his own head to snatch the ring in its mouth.

Fróech made a leap, too, and grabbed the fish by the gills. He brought it to land and hid it on the bank of the river. He began to climb out.

"Do not come out," said Ailill, "until you have brought me a branch from the rowan tree on the far bank. I think its berries are quite beautiful."

Frivolous though this request was, Fróech swam to the other shore, where he broke a branch from the tree and carried it back through the water.

After that day, whenever something struck her eye, Findabair would remark that even lovelier was the sight of Fróech in the dark water, his white skin wet, his hair sleek and gleaming, his shapely face with eyes of depthless blue, an altogether elegant youth without fault or flaw. His face was narrow below and broad above, symmetrical and perfect, and the branch with the red berries he carried in his teeth, between his throat and white face. Findabair used to say that she had never seen anything half or even a third as gorgeous as Fróech that day.

Fróech brought the branches to them from the water. "The berries are choice and lovely. Bring us more of them!" demanded Ailill.

Fróech went in again but, when he reached the middle of the pool, some kind of water-beast seized him. "Quick, throw my sword to me!" he cried.

Not a man dared respond for fear of Ailill and Medb.

Findabair caught up the sword, threw off her clothes, and plunged into the water.

Her furious father cast a five-pointed spear at her, which whistled between two tresses of her hair. Fróech caught the spear in his hand and tossed it back toward the riverbank while he also dealt with the monster. He deftly aimed the spear so that it passed harmlessly through both Ailill's crimson cloak and his under tunic. The warriors sprang up around Ailill, ready to protect him.

Findabair came out of the water, leaving the sword in Fróech's hand.

He cut off the head of the beast and brought it back to land. From that heroic incident, the waters are called the Dark Pool of Fróech in the river Bréi in the land of the Connachta.

Ailill and Medb retreated into their fort again.

"We have done an awful thing," said Medb, for Fróech was wounded.

"We regret what we have done to the man. As for the girl, however," Ailill raged, "her mouth will be stopped tomorrow night—although not for the crime of bringing the sword. Let us have a bath prepared for the man, a broth of fresh bacon with fresh beef chopped up by adze and axe, added into the bath."

Like bathing in healing soup, although it could have been made of horse, not pig or cow. I suspect the poets made it all up to tell the lying Welshman, Gerald of Wales . . . but that is another tale.

It was all carried out as commanded.

Fróech's horn-blowers preceded the wounded man through the crowd. They played so poignantly that thirty of Ailill's most valuable men died of sorrow.

Fróech entered the fort and flopped in the bath. A company of women surrounded the tub to rub him and bathe his head. He was brought out then and bedding was laid out.

Suddenly a racket, a wailing lamentation, filled the air at Crúachu. Three fifties of women approached the fort in procession, all wearing crimson tunics and hoods of green, with silver bracelets shaped like animals upon their arms. Messengers went to discover why they keened.

"For Fróech mac Idaith," said one woman, "young favorite of the king of all the *síde* of Ériu."

Fróech heard.

"Carry me out," he said to his troop. "My mother and the woman-troop of Boand are keening." He was carried out of the fort and brought to the women, who crowded around him and bore him away to the *síd* of Crúachu.

The next afternoon, at the ninth hour, Fróech returned with fifty exquisite women surrounding him. He was fully healed, once again without flaw or blemish. The women were all of the same age, equally beautiful, shapely, lovely, and graceful, and the look of the *síd* was on them, so that no one could tell one from another.

Well, that explains something: the fifty identical Étaíns.

Many men almost suffocated trying to press close to the women.

The women departed again through the gate of the enclosure, wailing as they went, and people fainted. That was when the musicians of Ériu first learned the wild cry of the banshee and its meaning.

Fróech entered the fort. All the hosts arose before him and welcomed him as if he had come from another world. Ailill and Medb also stood to greet him. They admitted their regret for the harm they had done to him, and everyone made peace. A feast was ordered for that night.

Fróech called a servant from his troop. "Go out," said he, "to the bank where I went into the water. I left a salmon there. Bring it to Findabair, entrust it to her, and let the salmon be well cooked by her. The ring is in the middle of the salmon. I think it likely that she will be asked for it tonight."

It was either his *síd*-nature that spurred this intuition or a glance at Ailill's stormy face.

They drank ale while musicians and other performers entertained them.

Ailill suddenly declared, "Let all my treasures be brought to me!"

They were brought and laid before him.

"Wondrously amazing!" everyone said when beholding the wealth of gold and silver and gems spread upon the ground.

"Call Findabair to me," said Ailill.

Findabair came to him with her fifty maidens around her.

"Daughter," said Ailill, "the ring that I gave you last year, do you still have it? Bring it to me so that I may see it. It will be yours again afterward."

Findabair hesitated. "I don't know what I did with it," she said.

"Find out," said Ailill. "Else your life will leave your body."

"It is not worth it," the young warriors cried out. "Look, there is enough wealth here already."

"I will give you anything on behalf of the girl," said Fróech, "for she brought me the sword to save my life."

"You have no treasure that can save her unless she restores the ring," said Ailill.

"I cannot do anything about it," sighed his daughter. "Do with me what you will."

"I swear by the gods that my tribe swears by, you will die if you do not give it back to me!" cried Ailill. "This is exactly why I asked for it, because it is impossible to return. Until all the men who ever lived from the start of the world should come back alive, the ring will not emerge from the place where it was cast."

Thus Ailill revealed his hand.

"It will not come back for wealth or wishing, certainly," said Findabair. "I must go seek it, since you ask so urgently."

"You will not go anywhere," growled Ailill. "Send someone else for it."

The girl sent her servant on the errand. She turned to her father and warned in a voice as cold as his, "I swear by the gods that my *túath* swears by, if the ring be found, I shall no longer be in your power, so long as another man will protect me."

"I shall not stand in your way, even if you run off with a stable boy, so long as the ring is found," said Ailill.

The serving maid arrived in the royal hall bearing a platter of salmon smeared with honey. Findabair had made it well. The golden ring lay atop the salmon.

Ailill and Medb were stunned.

"Give it to me so that I can look at it," said Fróech. Then he checked his purse. "Someone must have been watching when I took off my belt and purse," said Fróech. To Ailill: "Upon the meaning of your sovereignty, tell us what you did with the ring."

"I shall not keep it from you, then," said Ailill sullenly. "I knew my ring was in your purse, and I knew Findabair gave it to you. That is why I threw it into the dark pool. Upon your reputation and your soul, Fróech, tell how you arranged to bring it out."

"I shall not keep it from you," said Fróech. He told a little tale: "On my first day here, I found the ring on the ground in front of the enclosure. I knew it was a valuable treasure so I kept it safely in my purse. The first time I went down to bathe, I heard you asking for the ring. I noticed the girl looking for it. I asked her, 'What would reward would I get if I found it?' She told me that she would give me her love for a year. I did not have it on me just then, as I had left it behind in the house. We did not meet again until she brought me the sword in the river. I saw you open my purse and throw the ring into the water. I saw the salmon jump in front of me and catch it in his mouth. I caught the salmon, brought it onto the shore, and put it in the girl's hand. It is that same salmon on the dish."

The household marveled and wondered at the story. No one but Findabair knew which bits were untrue.

"I shall not look at any other man in Ériu but this one," said Findabair.

"Bind yourself to him," said Ailill and Medb, without even mentioning the outrageous bride-price they had demanded before. "Fróech, come to us for a raid into Cúailngne. The night when you return from the east with your cattle, that is the first night you shall spend with Findabair."

"I shall do so," promised Fróech. His company stayed until the next day. At dawn, Fróech and the troop readied themselves. He bade farewell to Ailill and Medb. No word on what he said to Findabair.

An easygoing man, Fróech. Ambushed by his future father-in-law, he and Findabair returned trick for trick. He was lucky to have *síd*-women to protect him.

A vengeful man, Ailill. More willing to execute his disobedient daughter than marry her off. Jealous of his wife, with good cause.

An easily swayed woman, Medb. Changeable. What was it that she once boasted? "I have never had a man without another man waiting in his shadow." Three nights of *fidchell* without a thought for anyone but Fróech, yet willing to murder him when Ailill devised a plan.

A brave maiden, Findabair, struck by Fróech's dark hair, blue eyes, white skin, and garland of rowan berries. Braver than any of her parents' men when she dared toss a sword to Fróech.

Would she have done it if she knew he was already married?

This is not the end of this tale.

Fróech and company set forth to their country to fetch his herds. Yet while he was away at Crúachu, his cattle had been stolen.

His mother came to him. "Your expedition was not so fruitful," said she. "It has caused a terrible problem. Your cattle, your three sons, and your wife were stolen away to

Slíab Alpa. Three of the cows were left in the north of Alba among the Cruithnech."

Slíab Alpa was the Alps, and the Cruithnech of Alba were Picts in Scotland.

"What shall I do?" he asked his mother.

"You must not seek them. You must not give up your life for them," said she. "I shall give you more cattle."

"Not so," said he. "I promised on my honor and soul to accompany Ailill and Medb, with my cattle, to raid Cúailnge."

You see, neither of them mentioned his wife and children.

"They cannot be found," warned his mother. She left him.

Fróech set forth nevertheless with three times nine men, a falcon, and a leashed hound. He traveled through a part of Ulaid where he met Conall Cernach at Benna Bairche (you might call them the Mourne Mountains, but they preferred the "The Peaks of the Peaky Area".) He put the matter to Conall.

"What's in store won't be good for you," said Conall. "Struggle and trouble awaits you—though it seems your mind is set."

"Help me. Come with me," pleaded Fróech, "now that we have met."

"Of course I shall go with you," said Conall Cernach. He never turned down a fight.

They set forth over the sea, thence across Britain, then over Muir nIcht—that is the Channel between Britannia and Frank-land—thence to northern Lombard territory in the Alps. Nobody liked the Lombards in those days. They had a dreadful reputation.

There the party came upon a servant woman herding sheep.

"Fróech, let us speak with that woman while the warriors wait here," advised Conall.

They went to speak to her.

"Where are you from?" she asked.

"From Ériu," said Conall.

"Surely, it won't be good for the men of Ériu coming here. My mother was from Ériu."

"Then help me because of our kinship. Tell us something about our situation: What kind of land have we come to?" Conall asked.

"A gloomy, terrible land with belligerent warriors. They dash all over the place, snatching cattle and kidnapping women and stealing treasure," said she.

"What did they get most recently?" asked Fróech.

"The cattle of Fróech mac Idaith from western Ériu, along with his wife and his three sons. His wife is kept by the king, and his cattle are right there, in the pasture before us."

"Help us," said Conall.

"I cannot do much, but I know a few things."

Conall said, "This is Fróech and they are his stolen cattle."

"Is the woman faithful to you?" she asked Fróech.

He considered. Did he think about Findabair?

"I trusted my wife before she was taken, but perhaps no longer, now that she is living here."

Could a woman's loyalties be so easily turned? Perhaps if her husband left home to seek another bride.

The shepherdess advised, "Go to the woman who tends the cattle. Tell her about your quest. Her people are from Ériu, too, from Ulaid, in fact."

They went to the cowherd and introduced themselves. She greeted them.

"What brought you?" asked she.

"Disaster," said Conall. "These are our cattle and our woman is inside the fort."

"It is risky to challenge the troop surrounding the woman," she warned, "and more dangerous still is the snake that guards the enclosure."

"I should not approach my wife directly," said Fróech, "for I do not trust her. I trust you, though. We know you will not betray us because you are from Ulaid."

"Who then is your man from Ulaid?" asked the woman, eyeing his partner.

"This is Conall Cernach, best warrior in the province," said Fróech.

The cowherd embraced Conall Cernach. "Destruction will certainly come to the fort now," said she, "because Conall's attack has been foretold. I must flee from here at once. I shall not even stay to milk the cows. Listen now: I usually close the gate to the enclosure when I come in, but I will leave it open this evening. I will say that the calves have sucked the cows already, and won't be straying this night. You should go into the fort when everyone is asleep. But beware of the snake that guards the fort, for it has felled entire tribes."

"We shall carry on, no matter what," said Conall.

That night, they attacked the enclosure. They razed the fort and rescued the woman and her three sons, and they took the best of the treasure from the fort. As for the snake, it slid into the belt of Conall Cernach at the start of the fight. At the end, it slid out again and departed with no harm to man or serpent.

Consider it as you will.

After that, they returned home by way of the Cruithnech, where they seized the three cows belonging to Fróech that were wandering among local cattle. They came past the Fort of Ollach Mac Briúin over the waters to Ard Úa nEchach in Conaille Muirthemne. One of Conall Cernach's servants died there, a cowherd named Bicne mac Láegaire. Since then, the place has been called the estuary of Bicne at Bennchor. As they led the cattle away from the water, the cows tossed their horns, so that place is called the Strand of Bennchor. (The pun is simple-minded: *benn* suggests horns and *cor* is throwing.)

Fróech went home with his wife and three sons and cattle. Later, he accompanied Ailill and Medb on the raid into Cúailnge, which is in Ulaid, where his friend Conall Cernach lived.

Yet Fróech died young, as was prophesied. During the Táin Bó Cúailnge, Medb sent him to kill Cú Chulainn while the latter was bathing in a river—a trick she had tried at home, you might recall—but the Cú proved too strong for Fróech as they wrestled in the water, and Fróech drowned there. His body was carried into the *síd* by a troop of green-cloaked women. This time, Fróech did not return. They named that *síd* after him and also the ford where he perished.

As for Findabair, she seems to have struck a bargain with Fróech. She saved him from the river monster and, in exchange, he saved her from her father. She was under Fróech's protection for a year. She had already given him the ring as her pledge. Whether they became man and wife, I cannot say. Medb continued to offer Findabair to other warriors as a prize for dueling with Cú Chulainn, but none of them survived. Findabair's fair face led to much slaughter.

Fróech's first wife never appeared again in stories, so perhaps she led a happier life.

"I swear, my deeds shall be celebrated among the champions' grandest exploits!"

THE SEVENTH TALE

Tochmarc Emire—The Courtship of Emer

YOU MIGHT SENSE THAT ONCE upon a time in Ériu, love was fickle, fragile, and fraught, and you would be right. Love interrupted peaceful marriages. Heroic husbands strayed and wives had little recourse but to practice their own secret adultery. If they were caught, women suffered harsher penalties than men. Medb was an exception. She selected and discarded men, one by one. There was one moment in their lives when other women might control the warriors of their affections: before they agreed to yield themselves.

Admittedly, sometimes they were not consulted in the negotiations, as in Étaín's first marriage. Some young women were traded to husbands like kine and swine on Beltaine at the start of summer. One maiden, as we know, was given away for her weight in gold and silver, not to mention projects of land clearance and river management. Then she spent centuries learning what to do with Midir.

The greatest hero in all of Ériu's history struggled long and hard to win a woman who held him at bay. She built a fortress of impossible demands around herself and set Cú Chulainn many arduous tasks before she went to his bed.

He adored nothing more than a challenge. Not even Emer. As the poet says, however, love dies young.

Once a noble and marvelous king ruled in Emain Macha, namely Conchobar son of Fachtna the Wise (although there were plenty of rumors that his father was really the druid Cathbad). More commonly they called him Conchobar son of Ness, who was his mother. He did great things while he ruled Ulaid. There was peace, calm, and merriment. There were abundant fruits of the wood, much game, and plenty of fish from the sea. There was order, law, and good lordship among the Ulaid during his reign. Great was the nobility, sovereignty, and abundance in the royal house of Emain.

That's not what Fergus said about Conchobar. Conchobar tricked Fergus out of the kingship and later killed some refugees who were under Fergus's protection. After that, Fergus left Ulaid to join Medb's armies and spend his nights in her tent. Fergus once said that Conchobar reduced his royal duties to three: watching the lads play hurley, playing *fidchell*, and drinking. But Fergus's story is for another time, as it is one bough of the great branch on our tree of tales, that is, the *Táin Bó Cúailnge*.

This is what the royal hall at Emain, called the Red Branch of Conchobar, looked like:

Nine rings of couches stretched from the central hearth fire to the outer wall. Each couch had a bronze partition, decorated with carvings of red yew, rising thirty feet tall. The house had a wooden floor and a roof of wooden tiles above.

Conchobar's compartment was at the front of the house, with ceiling slats of silver, held up by bronze pillars with glittering gold cornices adorned with carbuncles that flashed in the firelight, so that day and night were equally bright in the house. A plate of silver hung from the highest part of the royal house. When Conchobar struck it with his royal rod, all the Ulaid would turn to him and pay heed. Twelve couches for the best chariot warriors surrounded the central space.

Now, I wouldn't say it was shabbier than Medb's place, nor would I say it was shinier.

All the Ulaid warriors found a place in that royal house while drinking, without any crowding at all. They were noble, lordly, and good-looking men. The gatherings in that royal house were numerous and filled with wonderful entertainments. Performances and games and singing went on all the time. Warriors performed feats of strength and agility, poets chanted, and harpists and *timpán* players made splendid music.

One time the Ulaid warriors were gathered in Emain Macha with Conchobar, drinking beer from the enormous vat they called Iron-Gap. A hundred servings of drink filled the vat every evening, which satisfied all the Ulaid at the same time. The men would play at arms, balancing atop ropes stretched from one door to another in the hall at Emain. Fifteen feet plus nine score more was the diameter of the house. Three feats were performed there: the javelin feat, the apple feat, and the edge feat.

Cú Chulainn, youngest and newest of the company, had all these tricks in his repertoire.

So you can see how King Conchobar and his men spent their leisure at Emain. It was the duty of the ladies to keep the drink flowing no matter what. This was no mean task, but a noble duty for noble women. When Eochaid Airem selected Étaín from among fifty, didn't he test their skills at pouring ale? Queens learned how to fill a man's cup.

At that time, the men who showed their skills at Emain were Conall Cernach son of Amairgen, Fergus son of Roach the Brash, Lóegaire Búadach the Victorious son of Connad Buide, Celtchar son of Uithechar, Dubthach son of Lugaid, Cú Chulainn son of Súaltam (actually the son of Lug of the Túatha Dé), and Scél son of Bairdene (for whom the Pass of Bairdene is named) who was the doorkeeper of Emain Macha. From him comes the saying *Scél Scéoil* (Scél's Tale) for he was a great storyteller.

Cú Chulainn outshone them all at feats because he was born with prowess and agility. All the women of Ulaid loved Cú Chulainn the best because of his skill at feats, for his nimble leaps and twists, for the depth of his understanding, for the charm of his face, and for his dear expression.

He had seven pupils in his kingly eyes, that is, four pupils in one eye and three in the other. He had seven fingers on each of his hands and seven toes on each foot. He had plenty of other talents and gifts. The first gift was his wisdom—except, that is, when his warrior's frenzy came upon him. He had the gift of tricky feats. The gift of *buanfach*-playing (that was another board game). The gift of *fidchell*-playing. The gift of strategy. The gift of foresight. The gift of reason. The gift of manly beauty.

You might think that seven digits on each foot and hand would diminish his beauty, but not so in the eyes of the Ulaid men and women, not to mention more than one from the *síd*.

Cú Chulainn also had three faults back then: He was too young—his testicles were not fully descended yet, so strangers made fun of him. He was too bold. He was too good-looking.

The Ulaid had gathered for a council about Cú Chulainn, for all their women and daughters adored him. Cú Chulainn had no wife yet. The Ulaid decided that they must find a woman that he would agree to court, because a man with a suitable wife was less likely to make havoc among maidens or accept the love of other men's wives. Also, they feared Cú Chulainn's early death, which had been foreseen. They wanted him to get a wife and leave an heir. They knew well that it was only from a man like him that another would be born.

So nine messengers were sent from Conchobar to each province in Ériu to seek a woman for Cú Chulainn. They searched in every fort and settlement in Ériu for the daughter of a king, or a lord, or a landowner, or some other woman pleasing to Cú Chulainn that he might choose to court. Yet they returned a year later to Conchobar without finding a girl for Cú Chulainn.

So Cú Chulainn himself set out to woo a maiden whom he knew in Luglochta Loga, namely, Emer daughter of Forgall Monach.

Wait for it: did you notice the clues? Luglochta Loga was the Gardens of Lug, great king of the Túatha Dé and the Cú's secret you-know-what. Forgall's nickname was Wily. Clearly, this was not going to be a typical courtship. But then, what courtship is ever typical?

Cú Chulainn went with his charioteer, Lóeg Mac Ríangabra at the reins. The other horses could not keep up with their chariot, because of its splendid swiftness and the skill of those who drove it.

Cú Chulainn found Emer on the green with her foster sisters around her. They were daughters of the landowners attached to the fort of Forgall. The women were learning embroidery and handiwork from Emer. She was most worthy of Cú Chulainn among the women of Ériu, for she possessed six gifts: a fine manner, a lovely voice, sweet speech, skilled needlework, intelligence, and her virginity.

Cú Chulainn had said that he would take no woman from among the maidens of Ériu unless she was equal to him in age, manner, and ancestry. Emer was the only woman who had everything he wanted, so Cú Chulainn decided to woo her.

Wearing his best clothes, Cú Chulainn went that day to converse with Emer and show off for her. While the young women were sitting upon the ramparts during the men's assembly, they heard the noise of something swiftly approaching: the drum of horse hooves, the rumble of a chariot, the crack of the reins, the creak of wheels, the rush of the hero, the clank of weapons. "One of you look to see what is coming toward us," Emer suggested.

"Truly I see," said Fíal, another daughter of Forgall,

> *Two equally grand horses,*
> *both stunning, spirited, strong,*
> *sharp-eared, slim-headed, speedy,*
> *pricking their ears, stretching their lips,*
> *speckled all over, strapping and sturdy,*
> *and curly of mane and tail.*
> *One horse is grey,*
> *broad hipped, savage and swift,*
> *bounding along, thundering, pounding,*
> *crashing, clamorous,*
> *broad-breasted, broad-bottomed—*
> *the turf is afire where he hits the ground,*
> *he charges with four hooves flying,*

he outruns bird-flocks, casts off sparks,
he glows with fire and spits blood
as he chomps down hard on his bridle bit.
As for the second horse, it is gleaming black—

Here, I hope, Emer was sensible enough to ask her sister to get to the point. The adjectives suitable to war horses are not infinite. Suffice it to say, the second horse was as magnificent as the first, but it was a different color.

The young woman continued, "The chariot is made of wood and wicker, its wheels of bronze. The goad is of white silver tipped with white bronze. The framework, shiny and new, is of tin. The yoke is covered with thick gold plate. Its reins are fringed in yellow. Its steel spokes are straight as a blade.

"A dark, melancholy man rides in the chariot, most handsome of all men. A fine five-folded purple cloak surrounds him. A brooch inlaid with gold lies upon his pale breast, at the throat where his pulse beats. He wears a white hooded tunic, heavily embroidered with dazzling red-gold. Seven dragon-shaped red gems rest below each of his two eyes. His cheeks shine dark blood-red. They shoot off sparks and small fire-bursts. A ray of love sets his gaze aflame. I think a shower of pearls must have fallen into his mouth! Each of his brows is black as black can be.

"A gold-hilted sword rests at his thighs. A blood-red spearhead, well fit to hand, with a keen-edged blade on a shaft of dark wood, is caught to the copper framework of the chariot. A crimson shield with rim of silver, inlaid with animal figures of gold, hangs over his shoulders. He gives a heroic salmon leap, performing feats more deftly than any other, this chariot-warrior.

"There is a driver before him in the chariot, a slender, long-bodied, freckled man. Curly russet hair on his head, held back by a white-bronze fillet. Clasps of gold at the back of his neck, holding his plaits. He wears a mantle with sleeves to his elbows. A goad of red-gold in his hand to goad his steeds."

"Hmm," said Emer.

Fíal could have become a *ban-file* (woman-poet), if she wished.

Cú Chulainn arrived and greeted them. Emer lifted her fair-shaped face and recognized Cú Chulainn. She said politely, "I would drive southward for you," which was a greeting that meant, "May God smooth your way."

That was the manner in which high-born couples used to flirt. They spoke in poetic riddles. The bardic banter of Cú Chulainn and the object of his courtship was of such a high standard that no one can grasp all of it. It was a test of wit and experience devised to measure their mutual attraction. It was nothing like the crude talk of poles and seeds used by some men when wooing a woman.

"Safe is the pupil of your eye," said he, which meant, "May He keep you safe."

"Whence have you come?" she asked.

"From Emain today," said he.

"Where did you spend the night?"

"We spent the night with the man who catches the big fish of Mag Tethra."

"What did you eat there?" she said.

"The remains of a chariot were cooked for us," said he.

"How did you come?" said she.

"Between two woody ridges," said he.

"What way did you choose after?" she asked.

"Easy," said he, "from the Shelter of the Sea, by way of the Secret of the Túatha Dé, over the Foam of Two Horses of Emain, over the Field of the Morrígan, over the Backbone of the Great Sow, by the Glen of the Big Ox, between the God and his Seer, over the Marrow of the Woman Fedelm, between a Boar and His Mate, over the Wash of the Horses of Dea, between Ara's King and his Servant, thence to Mondchuile of the Four Corners of the World, over Aillbine the Great Crime, past the remains of the Great Brewing, between a Tub and a Smaller Tub, to the Daughters of the Nephew of Tethra, king of Fomoire, to the Gardens of Lug. So what is your tale, girl?"

If she was clever, and Emer was, she knew that he had come from Emain Macha, just south of Ard Macha to the estuary of the Bóinn, thence down the coast to Lug's Gardens, just north of Áth Cliath. She was nonplussed by his sudden question.

"Not hard to tell," she said. "I am the Temair of women, purest of maidens, wisdom of chastity. A vow unbroken. A watchman who does not see, a worm in water, a scaldcrow, some rushes left ungathered, Tethra of the Tethra. Daughter of a king, a flame of honor, a road never taken—in short, I am a chaste noblewoman and I have strong champions to guard me who will track down anyone who tries to abduct me without their permission and that of Forgall."

Cú Chulainn must have recognized her coded words, most of which proclaimed her virtue. Her last sentence was easier to understand. The hero realized that his quest would not be as easy as he had imagined.

"Who are the champions that guard you, maiden?" asked Cú Chulainn.

"Easy," said Emer. "Two Lui, two Lúath (Lúath and Láth Gaible son of Tethra), Tríath and Trescath, Brión and Bolar, Bas mac Omna, the eight Connlae, and Conn son of Forgall. Every one of them has the strength of a hundred men and performs the feats of nine men. Forgall himself has too many powers to reckon: he is stronger than any fighter, better trained than any druid, and clever as any poet. It will take more than all your feats to challenge Forgall himself, for his many powers and exploits are the stuff of epics."

"Why do you not count me among the champions, girl?" asked Cú Chulainn.

"If your deeds were sung about, would I not count you as one of them?"

"I swear, my deeds shall be celebrated among the champions' grandest exploits!"

You must be smiling. Cú Chulainn is the great hero of the *Táin Bó Cúailgne*.

"Right so. What can you do?" asked Emer.

"Wait for it," he said. "When I am weak, I can still protect twenty men. One third of my strength is enough to save thirty. My full fighting strength is enough to shield forty and to guard a hundred. My enemies avoid fords and battlefields for fear of meeting me. Troops and multitudes and masses of armed men run screaming at the sight of my face."

"Those are very nice accomplishments for a tender youth," smiled the maiden, "but you do not yet have strength of a chariot champion."

"Indeed! I was well raised by my foster father Conchobar. No ignorant rustic provided my education. I did not spend childhood between flagstone and kneading trough, nor between the hearth and the wall, nor on the ground of a single green. I was taught by Conchobar among many other chariot warriors and champions, among jesters and druids, among poets and wise men, and among landowners and farmers of Ulaid, so that I have *all* their ways and skills."

Ah, the lad took after his father, Lug the Many-Skilled. "Who among them taught you those great abilities of which you boast?"

"Not hard," said he. "Sencha the Smooth-Spoken taught me to be strong, sturdy, noble, and quick with a home thrust. I am wise in the laws. I am not forgetful. I can address any of the learned men. I attend to their words. I oversee the judgments of the Ulaid, but I do not alter them, all because of my training with Sencha.

"Blaí the Hospitaller accepted me, because of the closeness of our people, and gave me the privileges of food and shelter that he owed me as his lord, enough so that I can invite the fighting men of Conchobar's province, along with their king, to my feast for a week. I oversee their wealth and properties. I uphold their honor and collect fines.

"Fergus trained me to kill worthy warriors through valor and arms. I am fit, by myself, to guard the borders of our territory against strangers, for I am fierce in action with my weapons. I am a fortress for the weak; I am a weapon of destruction for the noble. I bring succour to the wretched; I make trouble for the oppressor. All because of my training with Fergus.

"Amairgen the Poet raised me so that I can praise every king appropriately, according to his rank, and so that I can match anyone in courage and contest, wisdom, wit, splendor, shrewdness, and spirit. I can challenge any chariot warrior, and I render tribute only to Conchobar.

"Finnchóem raised me to be co-fosterling with my near-equal, Connall Cernach the Victorious. Kind-faced Cathbad the Druid advised me for the sake of my mother, Deichtine, so that I am proficient in the study of the druids' arts, and also an expert among men of learning. So, in short, I was fostered by all the important Ulaid, both charioteers and warriors, both kings and chief poets. I am the darling of the war-bands and all the people, for I uphold the honor of everyone. Best of all, Lug Mac Cuinn meic Eithlenn acknowledged me as his son, following his encounter with Deichtine at the house of Burr in Brug na Bóinne."

Hush and I shall tell you something: Deichtine was the granddaughter of Óengus the Macc Óc.

Without pausing, Cú Chulainn asked, "But what about you, girl, how were you fostered in the Gardens of Lug?"

"I was raised according to our people's customs," said she, "with elegant behavior, incorruptible chastity, a queenly comportment, and a noble appearance. I was given all the best traits, about which so many other women boast."

"Those are fine customs, truly," said Cú Chulainn. "How could our union not be suitable? For I have not found until now a woman who could hold her own, one to one, in conversation with me like this."

"Wait. Do you have a wife?" asked the maiden, "To oversee your household for you?"

"I do not, in truth," said Cú Chulainn.

She thought about it. "No man gets my hand before my older sister marries," said the girl, "I mean Fíal daughter of Forgall, whom you see near me here. She is a model of handiwork."

"But I don't love her," complained Cú Chulainn. "Besides, I would not take a woman whom a man has already known. I heard that the girl once slept with Cairpre Nia Fer."

Let us hope that Fíal missed this conversation.

While they conversed, Cú Chulainn glimpsed Emer's cleavage peeking from her tunic. He said: "That is a beautiful plain, and a fine rack for resting weapons."

"No one approaches that plain," said she, "unless he slays at least a hundred at every ford, from the Ford of Scenn Menn at Aillbine to Banchuing Arcait—the White Yoke, where the Brea River hits Fedelm."

Cú Chulainn grasped her riddling names for stretches of the Bóinn River. "That's a beautiful plain for resting my weapon," he said.

"He shall not approach that plain," said the maiden, "unless he achieves the Salmon Leap, and strikes down three nines of men with one blow, while sparing the man in the middle of each nine."

"That plain is a lovely place to rest my weapon."

"He will not gain the plain unless he faces Benn Suain Mac Rosmilc from Samain to Imbolc, from Imbolc to Beltaine, Beltaine to Brón Trogan, that is, Lugnasad."

They were the four seasons of the whole year!

"It is said, it shall be done," swore Cú Chulainn.

"It is vowed, it is bound, it is received, it is agreed," said she. "Now a question: Who are you?"

"I am the nephew of the man who vanishes as another in the Wood of Badb," he said.

"What is your name, really?" asked she.

"I am the champion of plague that afflicts dogs," said he.

Cú Chulainn went away satisfied after those obscure words, and they had no more conversation that day.

While Cú Chulainn was on an expedition across Brega, his charioteer Lóeg asked him, "So, the words that you and the girl Emer exchanged, what did they mean?"

"Don't you realize that I am wooing Emer?" said Cú Chulainn, "We veiled our speech so that the girl-troop would not notice that I am courting her, for if Forgall found out, he would prevent us from meeting again."

Cú Chulainn then rehearsed the entire conversation for his charioteer, just to pass the time on their journey. "I said 'Intide Macha,' when she asked, 'How did you come?' I meant 'from Emain Macha: Macha, the daughter of Sainrith son of Imath, and wife of Crunniuc mac Agnomain, who was forced to run a race against the king's two horses when she was pregnant. She sped ahead and gave birth to a boy and a girl. From those twins—*emain*— Emain Macha is named, and the Plain of Macha is called after that same Macha.'"

Lóeg did not remind him that Macha brought the curse of labor pains upon the men of Ulaid. For five days and four nights the agony of birthing had them rolling on the ground in misery. Rightly so.

"Or," the Cú continued, "Emain Macha got its name as in this tale: Once, three kings jointly ruled Ériu. From Ulaid they came: Díthorbae mac Demain, in Uisnech in Mide; Áed Rúad mac Baduirn son of Bald Airget in Tír Áeda; and Cimbáeth mac Finntain son of Airgetmáil from Finnabair Maige nInis. It is he who fostered Ugaine Mór son of Eochaid Búadach. The men agreed that each would take the kingship for seven years. Three sevens of guarantors pledged to the oath sworn by them: seven druids with their endless incitements, the *filid* with their satirizing, mocking, and lampooning, and the lords who would wound and burn those who broke the agreement—that is, if one king did not give way to the next at the end of the seventh year, after maintaining good lordship—that is, no failure of the nuts and fruits every year, no lack of health, and none of the woman-troop dying during his reign."

The Cú did not tell which woman-troops he meant—Was it the noblewomen and wives? The nubile maidens? Camp followers? Fifty Étaíns?

"Each of the kings ruled for three terms in their turns over the next sixty-six years. Áed Rúaid died first of them when he drowned in Ess Rúaid, and his body was taken into the *síd*, hence the places are called Síd Áeda and Ess Rúaid. He did not leave any offspring except a daughter called Macha Mongrúad—Macha the Red-haired.

"She claimed the kingship in turn. Cimbáeth and Díthorbae would not yield the kingship to a woman. Fighting broke out among them and Macha vanquished the men. She spent seven years in the kingship. In the meantime, Díthorbae died in Corann. He left five fine sons: Báeth, Bras, Betach, Úallach, and Borbchas. They now demanded the kingship.

"Macha said she would not give it to them, as she put it, 'because I did not gain it by luck, but by force on the battlefield.'

"A fight broke out among them. Macha repelled the sons of Díthorbae and sent them into exile in the wilderness of Connacht.

"Next, Macha married Cimbáeth and made him chief of her troop of mercenaries.

"Once Macha and Cimbáeth were wed, Macha went hunting. Disguised as a leper, having plastered herself all over with rye dough stained red, she sought the sons of Díthorbae. She found them in the uncanny, rocky lands of Bairren Connacht (in the Burren) cooking a wild boar. The men asked her for news and she readily gave it. They offered food by the fire.

"One of them said to her, 'The eye of the old hag is beautiful, I shall sleep with her.' He brought her with him into the wood.

"She bound the man and left him among the trees, and then went back to the fire.

"'Where is the man who went with you?' they asked.

"'He was ashamed to come back,' she said, 'after he lay with a leper.'

"'There's no shame in it,' they said, 'we shall all do the same.'

"Each man took her to the woods. She bound them one at a time and then dragged them all bound together to Ulaid. The Ulaid said they should die.

"'Not so,' said she, 'for that would not be good lordship; but bound in slavery they shall dig a ring-fort around me and it will be the capital of the Ulaid forever.'

"With a pin she marked the perimeter of the fort for them, that is, with a brooch of gold at her neck, *muin*, and from that it is Emain Macha."

Cú Chulainn spoke the truth when he boasted of being a marvellous storyteller and speechmaker. He had certainly mastered the craft of the *filid*, as he had claimed to Emer. Not all of his tales were as fascinating as that of Macha.

He went on. "Now as to the route by which I came to Emer: The man I spoke of," said he, "in whose house we spent the night, that is the fisherman of Conchobar. His name is Roncu. He catches fish with a line in the sea, for the fish are cattle of the sea, and the sea is the plain of Tethra, who is a king of the Fomoire, the sea-people.

"The cookfire I mentioned, upon which the remains of a chariot were prepared for us—I was speaking of a foal. The chariot is forbidden to kings who have eaten a foal's flesh until three times nine days have passed. It is a *geis* to them.

"Concerning the passage between two woody ridges, they are the two mountains between which we drove, Slíab Fúait to our west and Slíab Cuilinn to our east. Between them is the wooded land called Oircél, The Pig Trough.

"By coming 'from the shelter of the sea,' I meant traveling from Mag Muirthemne. The sea covered it for thirty years after the Deluge, so it is a shelter or protection under the sea.

"Or this is why it is called Mag Muirthemne: a strange sea of druidry was once there that an armed man could sit on, as if on the ground. But the Dagda came with his Storm Club and recited certain words so that it receded.

"Amrún Fer nDea—the Great Secret of the men of Dea—is indeed a wonderful secret and mystery—today it is called Grellach Dolluid, Dollud's Marsh, for there Dollud son of Cairpre Nia Fer was run through by a boar. Before that, though, Amrún Fer nDéa was its name, for it was there that the Túatha Dé first planned for the Battle of Mag Tuired, because they refused the tribute that the Fomoire had imposed on them, that is, two-thirds of their grain, milk, and children.

"Over the Foam of the Two Horses of Emain: A famous young warrior, Nemed mac Nama, was king of the Goídil. He had two horses being raised at the *síd* of Eremon of the Túatha Dé. The two horses were loosed from the *síd* and an enormous flood burst after them. There was great foam atop that flood, which spread over the land for a year, so it was called 'foam on the water,' or Uanuib.

"What I called field of the Morrígan is Óchtar nEdmainn. The Dagda gave the land to the Morrígan and it was ploughed by her afterward. That year she killed Ibor Boichill son of Garb in her garden, and thereafter her garden only produced stinky pig fennel, because the son of Garb was related to her—it was a kin-slaying, worst of crimes."

It is not written whether faithful Lóeg responded to Cú Chulainn's monologue as they rumbled along. Perhaps he sighed. Or snored.

"Back of the Great Sow, well, that is clearly Druimm Breg. For every hill and mound in Ériu seemed to be shaped like a pig when the sons of Míl came to conquer Ériu, because the Túatha Dé Danann had laid a spell on the hills to make them hideous.

"The Glenn of Mardam it was called, that is Glend mBreogain today, after Breoga son of Breogund Sendacht, one of the sons of Míl. Mag mBreg was also named for him. It was called Glenn of the Great Dam, from Dam Dile son of Smirgall son of Tethra who was king of Ériu, and who once dwelt there. Dam died while escorting a company of Fodla's women when Mag Breg stretched all the way to the fort.

"The passage was called 'between the god and his seer,' that is, between Macc Óc in the Síd of the Brug and his seer, Bresal Bófháith from west of the Brug. A woman, wife of the smith, came between them. Anyway, that's the way we came, between the hill of the Síd of the Brug, which belonged to Óengus, and the Síd of Bresal the druid.

"Over the Marrow of the woman Fedelm, that is the Bóinn. This is why it is named the Bóinn: Boand wife of Nechtan mac Labrada went to guard the secret well at the bottom of the fortress with the three cupbearers of Nechtan, that is, Flesc, Lesc, and Luam. No one came back from the well unblemished unless he accompanied the cupbearers. The queen went with pride and haughtiness to the well, boasting that nothing would destroy her shapeliness or blemish her. She circled the well left-hand-wise to belittle its power.

Then three waves shot from the well and crashed over her, smashing her two thighs, her right hand, and one of her eyes. She ran from the *síd* all the way to the sea to avoid shame. Wherever she ran, the well ran after her. Segais was the well's name in the *síd*, the river Segsa, which runs from the *síd* to the pool of Mochua, the Arm of the wife of Nuadu and the Thigh of the wife of Nuadu after that, the Bóinn in Mide, Manchuing Archait it is called from Finda to the Troma, the Marrow of the woman Fedelm from Trom to the sea."

Apparently, the Cú knew a different story of Boand and the Bóinn than ours.

"The Triath, the Boar, called Cleitech and his mate Fésse. For *triath* is a name for a boar, chief of the herds. It is also a name for a king, chief of the tribe. What's more, Cleitech is the king—*cleith*—of a triumphant army. Fésse, indeed, is the name for the great sow, thus between boar and sow we came.

"The King of Ana, I said, and his servant, that is, Cerna through which we traveled. Síd Círinne was its name long ago but Cerna is now the name of the place. Enna Aignech killed Cerna, king of Ana, atop the mound and he killed Cerna's steward Gnia east of that place; thus it is forever known as Ráith Gníad in Cerna. Upon Gese, the king of the sons of Emne, Enna did that, because there was great friendship between Gese and Cerna.

"The Washing of the Horses of Dea, I said, today that place is called Ainge. But it was known originally as the *toinge* or *tonach* of the Gods' Horses, for it was there that the Túatha Dé first washed their horses after returning from the Battle of Mag Tuired. Ainge—"strong" or "crafty—it was called, after the king whose horses the Tuatha Dé Danann washed there.

"I said Four-cornered Mannchuile (Cetharchuile), that is, Muin Chuile. Mann the hospitaller was there. There was a great die-off of cattle in Ériu during the lordship of Bresal Brecc son of Fiachra Fobrecc of the Laigin. Mann dug large chambers deep under the earth in the place called Uachtar—Eight Corners—of Mannchuile. They were meant to protect against the plague. For seven years, he provided food for two dozen couples. Manchuile are the corners of Mann, so the place is Óchtur Muinchuile."

I am certain that Lóeg was rolling his eyes by then.

"Aillbine, so I said, the Great Crime—that is, the *síd* of Ailbine. There was a famous king here in Ériu, Rúad son of Rígdond from Munster. He attended a meeting with foreigners round the south of Alba, sailing in three ships, thirty in each. Their fleet was caught by something underwater while out to sea. They threw treasures and jewels into the sea, but the ships were not released. They drew lots to decide who among them should go underwater to find out what had stopped them. The lot fell to the king himself, so the king, Rúad Mac Rígduine, dove into the sea and disappeared. He came upon a great meadow where he found nine lovely damsels sitting. They admitted that they had halted the ships so that he would come to them. They would give him nine ships full of gold for staying nine nights and sleeping with one of them each night. He did thus. Meanwhile, his crews were unable to move because of the women's powers.

"One of the women said she would become pregnant by Rúad and bear his son, and he should return from the south to fetch the son. He returned then to his crew and they sailed off to spend seven years with their allies. They returned home afterward by another route that did not pass near that same plain. They reached the bay, Inber Ailbine. There the women met them. The men heard singing coming from the women's brass ship. While they anchored their fleet, the women came ashore and left the boy. The harbor was dark and rocky. Something happened to the boy on the stones and he died. The women swooned and called out 'Aillbine, Aillbine,' *oll-bine*, that is, a Great Crime. And from then on it was called Ailbine. Although another poem says that the woman chucked her own son out of the boat and onto the rocks. Shame!

"In Tresc in Máirimdill—Remains of the Great Feast— that is Taillne. It is there that Lug Scimaig made a great feast for Lug Mac Ethlenn to comfort him after the Battle of Mag Tuired. That was his inauguration feast as king, for the Túatha Dé made Lug their king after Núada was killed. The place where they threw their refuse made a great hill. It was Hill of the Great Feast or Remains of the Great Feast, that is, Taillne today.

"Concerning the daughters of the nephew—*nia*—of Tethra, well, Forgall Manach, king of Fomoire, is a nephew of Tethra. *Nia* is a sister's son or nephew and *nia* is also the word for a mighty warrior.

"Surely you understand the bit about myself that I told her: There are two rivers in Crích Roiss. Conchobar is the name of one, and Dofolt (that is, Hairless) is the name of the other. Conchobar flows into the river Dofolt and mingles with it, so that they become one water there. I am the nephew of Conchobar, son of Deichtine, sister of Conchobar. Or I am *Nia*, a champion of Conchobar.

"Ross Bodba is Wood of the Badb, that is, the Morrígan. For the woody territory of Crích Roiss is hers, and she is called the Badb or Scaldcrow of battle, and she is also Bé Néit, the goddess of battle, for she is wife of Néit, the god of battle.

"What about the nickname I gave myself, the hero— Núada—of the plague that befalls dogs? The plague of rabies is wild and ferocious. I am a mighty carrier of that ferocious plague; that is, I am fierce and rabid in battles and skirmishes.

"When I said, 'Fair that plain of the Noble Yoke—Mag Alchuing,' I did not really mean a plain like Mag mBreg, but the girl's own body. For I saw her two breasts through an opening in her shift, so I said 'Mag Alchuing' to mean her breasts.

"Now, when she said, 'No one reaches that plain unless he kills as many as *argat*,' well, *argat* is a hundred in the language of poets, so it meant that I cannot carry off the girl unless I kill a hundred men at each ford from Ailbine to the Bóinn together with wily Scennmenn, her paternal aunt, who will shift into any shape to destroy my chariot and kill me," said Cú Chulainn.

"'Geni Grainde,' she said, meaning she would not come away with me until I made salmon leaps over three ramparts to fetch her—for she has three brothers guarding her, Ibur, Scibur, and Catt, each in a troop of nine men. I must strike a blow upon each troop so that eight of them die without harming any of her brothers. Then I shall take her and her co-fosterling, along with their weight in gold and silver, away from the fort of Forgall.

"'Benn Súain son of Rosc Mele,' she said, meaning that I shall fight without getting hurt from Samain—that is the end of summer (*sam-fuin*.) For long ago they used to divide the year into just two seasons, summer from Beltaine to Samain, and winter from Samain to Beltaine. Or else *samfuin* includes *suain* (sounds), for summer has gentle sounds, *sam-són*.

"And Imbolc or Oimelc, the beginning of spring, is *ime-folc*, different-wet; that is, the wetness of spring and wetness of winter. Or *oí-melc*, a poetical way of saying sheep, and from this it is said *oíba*, plague or death of sheep—similar to *coinbá*, death of dogs; *echba*, death of horses; *duineba*, death of men, for *bá*, *bath* means 'death'. *Oimelc* is the when the sheep come out to be milked, for *oísc* is an ewe.

"And Beltaine, that is *bil-tine*, fortunate fire, for the druids made two fires with great incantations and every year they drove the cattle between them to prevent diseases. Or *bel-dine*, for Bel indeed is the name of an idol and a god. The young of every herd was presented to Bel. *Beil-dine* is Beltaine.

"Until Brón Trogain, that is, Lugansad, Lammas-day, the beginning of autumn. It is then that the earth suffers— *do-broini*—as it bears fruits, for *trogan* is another name for *talam*, earth. But everyone really called it Lugnasad in honor of Lug."

With that, long-winded Cú Chulainn and the dazed Lóeg proceeded to the feast at Emain Macha that night.

His method of courting a woman is not one much used now except, perhaps, by a few pedants such as authors of dictionaries.

The young women at Forgall's house told all their fathers about the young warrior who had come in his fine chariot and the conversation that he and Emer had carried on between themselves. No one knew what the two had declared to each other, or that the warrior had turned northward across Mag Breg.

The landowners told Forgall Manach everything, including that his daughter had spoken with the young warrior.

"It is true," said Forgall Manach, "the Warped One from Emain Macha came here to speak to Emer. The girl loves him and that is why they spoke together. But that will not help them. I shall prevent them from getting what they want."

Everyone called Cú Chulainn the Warped One. He was literally *ríastarthae*—the contorted, stretched, warped one—when he was set aflame by the inner furor of battle lust. This is what happened to him when he entered his warp-spasm: He expanded to enormous size, trembling while his legs reversed, so that his feet faced backward. One of his eyes sank into his head and another popped out on its stalk. His mouth reached his ears and he blew out fire while a geyser of blood shot from his head, while his hair formed a kind of mist around his head. No one could withstand Cú the Ríastrathae.

Forgall Manach decided to go to Emain Macha dressed in foreigners' clothing, as if he were a messenger from the king of foreigners, sent to speak with Conchobar concerning the golden treasure of the Finn Gall and other riches. He came with two others, and they were made very welcome. When he sent away his men on the third day, Cú Chulainn and Conall and all the other chariot-warriors of the Ulaid were praised in Forgall's presence. He agreed that the performance of the warriors was wonderful, but that if Cú Chulainn went to Domnall Míldemail across the mountains in Alba, he would be even better at feats; and if he went to Scáthach, the Shadowy One, to learn the arts of war, he would surpass all the champions of Europe.

But in fact, he proposed this to Cú Chulainn so that the young hero would never come back. Forgall believed that if Cú Chulainn made a union with Emer, that he, Forgall, would die somehow, given the hostility and fierceness of the warrior. His solution was to make Cú Chulainn disappear.

Cú Chulainn vowed to go forth and train, and Forgall bound himself with sureties, promising that if the Cú went at once, he would get whatever he desired as a reward. Forgall went home. The warriors arose the next day and set about their vow. Cú Chulainn and Lóegaire Búadach and Conchobar went off together. Some say that Conall Cernach went, too.

Cú Chulainn crossed Brega to visit Emer before boarding his ship. The girl revealed to him that it was Forgall who had urged him, in Emain, to go and train in warfare so as to keep him from seeing her. And she told him to beware, for Forgall would try to destroy Cú Chulainn wherever he went. They both promised to remain chaste until they met again, unless threatened with death. They bade farewell to each other and the Cú turned toward Alba.

When the warriors found Domnall Míldemail, he taught them to blow the bellows through a hole in a flagstone. They performed feats on the stone until the soles of their feet were dark or livid from the heat. Another feat they learned was to climb their spears and perform a trick on the spear-tip called the Binding of Champions, without piercing their feet and bleeding.

Domnall's daughter fell in love with Cú Chulainn. Dornalla was her name, Large-fisted Dornalla. Her appearance was dreadfully ugly, for her knees were huge, her heels turned to the front, and her toes to the back. She had big greyish-black eyes and her face was black as jet. Her forehead stuck out, and her coarse bright red hair was caught with a headband.

Cú Chulainn refused to share a bed with her. She swore her revenge.

Domnall said that Cú Chulainn's training would not be complete until he went to Scáthach, who lived east of Alba.

So four of them went forth across Alba: Cú Chulainn and Conchobar king of Ulaid and Conall Cernach and Lóegaire Búadach.

Suddenly, a vision of Emain Macha rose before their eyes. Conchobar and Conall and Lóegaire could not go any farther. The daughter of Domnall had cast that vision upon them so as to separate Cú Chulainn from his comrades, in order to destroy him.

Another storyteller claims that it was Forgall Manach who put the illusion on them in order to turn them back, so that Cú Chulainn would not be able to fulfil the vow made in Emain, and would be shamed. Or, if he went eastward to learn feats of arms—both common and extraordinary—from Scáthach, he would be likely to meet death on his own.

Cú Chulainn chose to go his own way on an unfamiliar path. The girl's powers were indeed great, for she brought danger upon him by separating him from his band. As Cú Chulainn made his lonely way across Alba, he was gloomy and troubled by the loss of his companions. He did not know how he would find Scáthach. He had pledged to his companions that he would not return again to Emain unless he reached Scáthach or was killed. He stayed a bit in one place lest he go astray.

While he was halting there, he suddenly saw a dreadful monster like a lion coming toward him. It watched him yet did not attack. Whichever way he went, the beast got in front of him, turning its side to him as if to halt him. He took a chance and leaped on its back. He did not try to guide it, just went with the beast wherever it wanted. For four days they traveled in that manner until they came to an inhabited territory and a lake where a boy-troop was rowing. The lads laughed in delight to see the dangerous monster in servitude to a man. Cú Chulainn jumped down then and the beast left him. He saluted it.

Cú Chulainn continued until he came upon a large house in a great valley. Inside the house he found a good-looking young woman. The girl greeted him.

"Your coming is welcome, Cú Chulainn," said she.

He asked how she knew him.

She reminded him that they had been co-fosterlings with Ulbecán the Saxon. "When I was there, you were learning sweet speech from him." The girl brought him drink and a bite to eat, and then he left her.

He met a brave young warrior there who welcomed him in the same way. They exchanged news. Cú Chulainn sought information about the fortress of Scáthach. The warrior gave directions for crossing the plain of bad luck that was first on his route. He said that on the near side of the plain, men's feet froze to the ground. On the far side of the plain, the grass would rise and stick them on tips of its blades. The warrior gave Cú Chulainn a wheel and told him to walk in the wheel's track across the first half of the plain, so he would not get stuck. He also gave Cú Chulainn an apple, telling him to follow wherever the apple rolled across the far half of the plain, so as to avoid getting caught by the grass.

In that way, Cú Chulainn crossed the plain and kept going.

The warrior had also mentioned a great valley that lay ahead, with one narrow track through it that was full of monsters sent by Forgall to destroy him. That was the way to Scáthach's house, across the perilous rocky heights.

Eochaid Bairche was that youth. He and Cú Chulainn saluted each other after Eochaid taught him how to win honor in Scáthach's house. The same young warrior prophesied that he would sustain struggles and hardship on the Cattle-raid of Cúailnge. He also foretold the evils and exploits and triumphs that the Cú would someday inflict on the men of Ériu.

So Cú Chulainn set out on the road that led across the plain of misfortune and through the terrible valley, just as the young warrior had instructed. That is how Cú Chulainn reached the fort where Scáthach's pupils were gathered. He asked them where she was.

"On the island yonder," said they.

"What way do I go to her?

"By the Bridge of Recruits," they answered, "but no one crosses until he is skilled with arms."

The bridge had two low heads and a raised middle, so that when someone leaped upon one end, the other end sprang up and threw him on his back.

Some tellers insist that a multitude of warriors from Ériu were there in the fort learning feats with Scáthach, namely, Fer Diad mac Damáin, and Noíse mac Uislenn, Lóchmor mac Egomais, and Fiamain mac Forai, and loads of others.

But not in this tale.

Cú Chulainn tried to cross the bridge three times and failed. The recruits mocked him. Cú Chulainn's war-frenzy caught him then. He vaulted onto the head of the bridge, then made his famous salmon leap and landed in the middle of the bridge. Cú Chulainn jumped again to the end of the bridge before it could spring up, and he landed on the island.

He went to the fort and knocked so hard with his spear that it pierced the gate.

Scáthach was alerted. "Truly," she said, "this is someone who has finished his warrior training elsewhere." She sent her daughter Úathach to find out who the lad was. Úathach looked him over, but she could not speak because his beauty overwhelmed her with desire. She finished staring and returned to her mother to praise the man.

"The man pleased you, then," said her mother. "I see it on you."

"That is entirely true," admitted the girl.

"Then take him to bed and sleep with him tonight if that is what you want."

"No problem there, if he wants it, too," said she.

The girl attended him, bringing water and food, entertaining him and seeing to his pleasure. She approached him boldly, like a serving girl. Cú Chulainn pounced on her but accidentally hurt her finger, so she screamed. Everyone in the place came running.

Cochar Cruifne, the champion battle-warrior of Scáthach, came at Cú Chulainn, and they struggled for a long time. Scáthach's champion relied on all the martial skills he had learned, but Cú Chulainn gave as good as he got, as if he had learned all the same tricks as a lad. Cochar fell by Cú Chulainn's hand, and the Cú took his head.

Scáthach was not happy about it, but Cú Chulainn offered to take on the labors and duties of the man he had defeated. He would become her champion and the leader of her troops.

After that, Úathach came back to Cú Chulainn.

Perhaps her finger seemed a petty problem after watching Cú Chulainn take down Cochar.

On the third day, she advised him that, if he had come to learn warriors' skills, he should use the salmon leap to reach the place where Scáthach was instructing her two sons, Cúar and Cett, in the great yew tree. He should place his sword between Scáthach's breasts and make three demands: full instruction in fighting; a dowry for marriage; and to reveal what would befall him in future, for Scáthach was a seer.

So Cú Chulainn followed Scáthach. He jumped atop the basket of weapons, unsheathed his sword, and set its edge against her chest. He said, "Death hangs over you."

"I will grant three demands," said she, "if you can ask them in one breath."

"Agreed," said he. He recited his demands and secured her oath.

Other versions say that Cú Chulainn brought Scáthach down onto the strand to have sex there, and she recited his future to him, chanting, "Welcome, weary victorious one," and so on.

But that is not the version told here.

Úathach stayed with Cú Chulainn after that, while Scáthach taught him warfare and weaponry.

While Cú Chulainn stayed with Scáthach and her daughter, another famous man from Mumu—namely, Lugaid mac Nóis, a foster brother of Cú Chulainn—went from the west with twelve lesser kings of Mumu, to woo the twelve young daughters of Cairpre Nia Fer, son of Russ Ruad. But all the maidens were already betrothed to other men. When Forgall Monach heard about it, he hurried to Temair. He told Lugaid that he had in his household an unmarried, chaste woman, the best in Ériu, the shapeliest, most virtuous, and best housewife. Lugaid was pleased to learn it. Forgall betrothed Emer to the king, and twelve daughters of landowners from Brega were betrothed to the twelve lesser kings abiding with Lugaid.

King Lugaid came with Forgall to his fort for the wedding feast. But when Emer was brought to sit next to Lugaid, she clutched his two cheeks and swore on his honor and life that she loved Cú Chulainn and was under his protection, and that it would violate her honor if she were given to anyone else. Lugaid did not sleep with Emer that night for fear of Cú Chulainn. He returned home again, unmarried.

At the time, Scáthach was at war with other tribes whose ruler was Aífe. The two armies prepared to do battle. Scáthach gave Cú Chulainn a sleeping draught and ordered that he be tied up, so that nothing could happen to him in battle. She was taking a precaution. But Cú Chulainn awoke, fresh and ready, after only an hour, and burst his bonds. Anyone else who swallowed the drink would have slept the whole day.

Cú Chulainn went with the two sons of Scáthach to face three of Aífe's soldiers, that is, Cúar, Cett, and Cruife, the sons of Ilsúanach. He fought the three of them alone and cut them down. The real battle began the next day. The two hosts arrayed themselves face to face. Three more soldiers of Aífe, the three sons of Éis Enchenn the Birdheaded—Ciri, Biri, and Blaicne—challenged the two sons of Scáthach to fight.

They chose to duel on the Rope of Feats. Scáthach let out a sigh, for she feared the outcome. Her sons did not have a third man with them, so it was two against three. What's more, Aífe was the fiercest woman-warrior in the world. But Cú Chulainn joined her two sons and leapt upon the Rope. By himself he fought the three men and slaughtered them.

Aífe challenged Scáthach to a duel. Cú Chulainn sought out Scáthach to ask what Aífe loved best. Scáthatch said,

"What she loves best are her two horses, her chariot, and her charioteer."

Cú Chulainn instead of Scáthach met Aífe on the Rope of Feats. Aífe broke Cú Chulainn's sword, leaving him with nothing but the hilt. Cú Chulainn quickly cried out, "Oh-oh, look! Aífe's charioteer with her two horses and the chariot have fallen into the glen! They're all dead!"

Aífe looked where he pointed and Cú Chulainn jumped her. He seized her by the breasts, then tossed her over his shoulder like a full bag, and carried her back to Scáthach's army. He dumped her on the ground and held a naked sword over her.

"A life for a life, Cú Chulainn," Aífe pleaded.

"I have three demands," said he.

"You shall have whatever you can ask in one breath," she promised.

"Here are my three demands: Send hostages to Scáthach as a pledge that you will not attack her again; sleep with me tonight at your fort; and bear me a son."

"I agree to all your demands," said she, "and thus it shall be done."

Cú Chulainn accompanied Aífe and slept with her that night. Afterward, Aífe declared that she was pregnant and carrying a boy. "I will send him to you in Ériu on this day, seven years from now," she told him, "but you must name him."

Cú Chulainn gave her a golden ring and declared that the boy should seek him in Ériu when the ring fit the growing child's finger. He added that the name of the boy should be Connlae. Aífe should teach him never to reveal him name, never to yield the road, and never to refuse a fight.

Afterward, Cú Chulainn returned to his allies in the same way he had come, meaning, I suppose, by the Rope of Feats. He met an old woman, blind in the left eye, on the path. She demanded that he give way. He refused because that would cause him to fall off the Rope and down the cliff. She demanded that he yield. So he gave way and clung by his toes to the Rope. As the hag went past, she stepped on his big toe to knock him off, but he sprang up in his salmon leap and cut the hag's head off. She was Eis Enchenn the Bird-headed, mother of the three warriors whom he had recently massacred. She had come for him to avenge her sons and destroy him.

After that, the army of Scáthach went to their own territory, bringing the hostages sent from Aífe. Cú Chulainn stayed a while to heal his wounds.

He had finished his training in military feats with Scáthach—learning the apple feat, thunder-feat, blade-edge feat, the leveled shield feat, the spear feat, the rope feat, the body feat, the feat of Cat, the salmon leap of a chariot-warrior, the throwing of poles, the leap into the air, the brave warrior's crouch, the secret *gae bolga*, the spurt of speed, the wheel feat, the shield rim feat, the breath feat, the cry-crushing feat, the hero's whoop, the careful strike, the stunning strike, the shriek-strike, the climbing of a flying lance and standing on its tip, the sickle chariot, and the binding of a warrior on the points of spears.

Finally, a message called him back to his own country. He bade everyone farewell. Before he went, though, Scáthach revealed his future. She chanted for him through the *imbas forosnaí*—the inspiration of foresight. It was the greatest talent of any *fáith* or *fili*, prophet or poet—a magical skill extremely difficult to cultivate.

She sang these words to him:

> *You will always be a lone warrior*
> *Whom a world of danger awaits,*
> *It's you against an endless herd.*
> *Heroes prepare to fight you,*
> *You will snap their greedy gullets,*
> *Cutting your backward slash,*
> *Blood spurts will shower Sétanta.*
>
> *A sharp-edged club as witness,*
> *Warnings carved in raw flesh,*
> *Your herds are driven away,*
> *Hostages seized from your tribe.*
> *Tears shall rain for two weeks,*
> *While your cattle wander the passes.*
>
> *Just one against the reavers*
> *Your blood spatters battered shields*
> *Like a river of bloody plague.*
> *You will track the flea-bitten band,*
> *The ones who lead the hordes,*
> *Then eruptions of blood will color*
> *The skin and bones of Cú Chulainn.*
> *Ignoring the bruises and gashes,*
> *Prepared for the final breach*
> *Your bloody spear-tips blunted,*
> *Yet afire against the torrent*
> *Surging over the battle champion,*
> *the lad with a thousand feats.*

Wailing women will strike.
Ailill and Medb will squabble.
You shall tumble into a sickbed,
Injured, broken, suffering.

I can see the sleek Findbennach
against the bawling Donn of Cúailnge.
et cetera.

And so on. That is the shorter version of Scáthach's
Words. You can find much longer versions, with many
more blood-soaked phrases, in other books. They tell of Cú
Chulainn's trials during the great *táin* brought by Ailill and
Medb, and hint at other adventures of the hero of heroes—
his duels with the greatest warriors whom, of course, he
overcame; the wounds, gorings, stabbing, slicings, cleavings,
and beheadings that he wreaked; and the women that he left
unhappy. Enjoy yourself.

Foresight was the privilege of poets, druids, and female
seers, as well as a few Christian saints. Some were born with
the skill. Others spent years practicing, not just trying to
summon the future on command but also learning how to
explain their visions to others. The form that they usually
chose was extremely obscure poetry full of ambiguous hints,
as Scáthach did.

After the Shadowy One finished her prophecy, Cú Chulainn
boarded a ship to Ériu. With him went Lugaid and Lúan, two
sons of Lóeg, and Fer Boeth, Láirin, Fer Diad, and Drust mac
Seirb. They reached the house of Rúad, king of the Isles, on
the eve of Samain. Conall Cernach and Lugaid Búadach were

there levying dues, for at that time the foreigners of the islands paid dues to the Ulaid.

Cú Chulainn heard the sound of grieving coming from the king's fort.

"What is that lament?" asked Cú Chulainn.

"The daughter of Rúad is being given as tribute to the Fomoire," they said, "that is why you hear them lamenting."

"Where is she?" asked Cú Chulainn.

"She is below on the strand," they said.

Cú Chulainn found the girl on the beach and asked for her story. The girl told him the whole thing.

"Whence do the men come?" asked he.

"From that island in the distance," said she, "But do not wait here to see the reavers."

Yet he remained there to face them, as one would expect of Cú Chulainn. He killed the three Fomoire all by himself. The last of them wounded the Cú's wrist before falling. The girl bandaged him with a strip of her skirt. He left without telling his name.

The girl went to the fort and told her father everything. Then Cú Chulainn came to the fort as did other guests. Conall and Lóegaire welcomed him. Many men took credit for killing the Fomoire, but the girl did not believe any of them.

The king had a bath prepared and each man was brought in his turn to it, so that she could have a look. Cú Chulainn took his turn and the girl recognized him.

"I shall give my daughter to you," said Rúad "and a dowry with her."

"Not so," said Cú Chulainn, "let her come after me to Ériu in a year to the day, if that be her wish, and she will find me there."

Cú Chulainn returned to Emain after a while and told of his adventures. When he had rested, he went to Forgall's fort to seek Emer. For an entire year he skulked near the fort, but he could not even glimpse her because she was under watch.

At the end of a year he said, "Today, Lóeg, we shall tryst with the daughter of Rúad—but I do not know exactly where, for I was not smart enough to set a place. Go with me to the borderlands."

When they arrived on the banks of Loch Cúan, they saw two swans soaring over the sea. Cú Chulainn put a stone in his sling and shot at the birds. He hit one and the two men ran after it. When they reached the birds, though, they found two of the most beautiful women in the world. There was Derb Forgaill, the daughter of Rúad, and her maid.

"You did something evil, Cú Chulainn," said she, "for we came seeking you, but you have injured us."

Cú Chulainn knelt and sucked the stone out of her side along with a mouthful of blood.

"Sadly, I cannot ever be with you," said Cú Chulainn, "as I have tasted your blood. I shall give you to my foster son, Lugaid Riab nDerg, instead."

And that was that, as we shall see in Derb Forgaill's own tale.

Cú Chulainn headed back to Forgall's fort, but he was still unable to approach the girl because they watched her so intently. The next day he decided to go directly to the house of Forgall. His sickle chariot was readied for him that day. They called it his sickle chariot because of iron sickles, like spikes, that stuck out from it (or else it was invented by

Sickle-people.) He also readied himself by practicing three hundred and nine thunder feats beforehand.

He finally arrived at Forgall's fort and, right away, he performed a salmon leap over the three enclosing walls, landing on the ground in front of the house. Then he struck three blows, so that eight men fell at each strike, while the one man in the middle of each nine stayed safe—that is, he spared Scibur and Ibur and Cat, three brothers of Emer.

Forgall leapt over the ramparts trying to flee Cú Chulainn, but he fell to his death. Cú Chulainn caught up Emer and her foster sister, along with their weight in gold and silver, and sprang back over the three walls of the fort. They rushed away while the alarm was raised everywhere. Forgall's sister Scenmenn attacked them, but Cú Chulainn killed her at a ford, so that now they call it the Ford of Scenmenn.

They pushed on to Glondath, where Cú Chulainn killed another hundred men.

"You performed a great heroic deed—a *glond*," said Emer, "killing a hundred armed men here."

"This place will be named the Glond-áth, Ford of Great Deeds forever," he responded.

They reached Crúfóit. Before that, its name was Ráe Bán or White Field. Cú Chulainn struck massive deadly blows to the troop gathered at that place, so that rivers of blood flowed all around.

"Now there is a turf of blood, *fót cró* on this hill today," said Emer.

The place is now Crúfóit.

Imagine that—even amidst ceaseless attacks and desperate flight, the Cú and Emer took time for the wordplay of landscape and courtship.

Their pursuers caught up to them at Áth nImfúait over the Bóinn. Emer hopped out of the chariot. The horses kicked up clumps of sod to the north as Cú Chulainn led the pursuit northward. Then he turned them and the sods from the horses' hooves rained southward. So the place is called Áth nImfúait, the Ford of Strewn Sods, from the clumps of turf all over the place.

That is how Cú Chulainn killed a hundred at every ford from Áth Scenmenn on the Aillbine to the Bóinn at Breg and fulfilled his promises to the girl. They continued safely after that and reached Emain Macha at nightfall.

Emer was conducted into the hall and before Conchobar and the nobles of Ulaid, and they welcomed her. However, the one dour, evil-tongued Ulsterman in the house, Bricriu son of Carbad, said, "What happens tonight will bring big trouble for Cú Chulainn. His new wife will have to sleep with Conchobar tonight, for he always deflowers the virgins before the husband."

Cú Chulainn went crazy when he heard that, shaking so violently upon his seat cushion that it burst and feathers flew all over the house. He stormed outside.

"It is indeed a great difficulty," said Cathbad, "for it is a required by custom that the king do what Bricriu says. Yet Cú Chulainn will kill anyone who sleeps with his wife."

"Let Cú Chulainn be called to us," said Conchobar, "so we can try to ease his anger."

Cú Chulainn returned to the house. "Come here to me," Conchobar said, "and bring with you the herds on Slíab Fuait."

Cú Chulainn went out and drove before him the pigs he found on Slíab Fuait, and the wild deer, and every type of wild game, and herded them in a single flock to the green before Emain. The work diminished Cú Chulainn's fury toward Conchobar.

The Ulaid consulted together about the problem. They decided that Emer should sleep with Conchobar that night, but Fergus and Cathbad would sleep in the same bed with them to preserve Cú Chulainn's honor (and that of Emer, one supposes), and thus all would be well with the Ulaid and their customs, if Cú Chulainn agreed. He agreed and it happened thus. Conchobar paid Emer's dowry the next day and Cú Chulainn's honor-price. The Cú slept with his wife after that and they never separated until death found them both.

Or so the story goes, but it was not entirely true. They never separated or divorced, but Cú Chulainn did go his own way rather often, leaving Emer behind at home. Besides his antics while training with Scáthach, there was that time during the great cattle raid when he once more promised Emer that he would remain chaste while he—but never mind, that is another tale for another time.

"Every tryst in this world leads to longing…"

THE EIGHTH TALE

Aided Derbhfhorghaill—The Death of Derb Forgaill

WHEREVER CÚ CHULAINN WENT, HE seemed to leave melancholy females behind. If one of his lovers followed him home to Ulaid, the consequences were disturbing, as the last two tales in this book make clear.

Yet what else, I ask you, could one expect of a lad destined to be the greatest warrior who ever lived? Ladies loved him. After all, Cú Chulainn, who was first named Sétanta, took up arms at the age of seven. He gained his nickname by slaying a vicious guard dog (do you know how big wolfhounds can grow?) and taking its place as the Hound of Culann. He played hurley with human heads and danced on the tips of spears. He defended the borders of Ulaid by himself on his very first day as an armed warrior, slaughtering three grown fighters and bearing trophies to King Conchobar at Emain Macha. So frenzied and furious was the lad as his chariot rumbled to the gate that Conchobar cried, "Send women to him!" and the ladies of Emain Macha rushed outside to calm and shame Cú Chulainn by revealing their snowy breasts. They sometimes had to dunk the lad in three cauldrons of cold water, one after the other, before he settled down, as we shall see.

A woman's skin, her touch, her delicate face, her alluring words were the only things that could drag Cú Chulainn's mind from combat, or training for combat, or recovering from combat. Perhaps that is why he took so many lovers. But he had only one wife and that was Emer, daughter of Forgall Manach, whom he struggled to win. Emer was only jealous once, as one of the tales reminds us. Yet she was clever, so perhaps she pretended to believe him when he swore fidelity.

One could spend a year telling tales of Cú Chulainn—how he could heave a spear and then race his chariot so swiftly that he caught his weapon before it landed. How he could lop the heads off three men with one blow. How he won Emer by slaughtering entire companies of men. How he alone held off the allied armies of Ériu led by Medb to steal the Brown Bull, by dueling its best fighters one by one. He had countless talents, feats, and tricks, including the *gae bolga*, that vicious, mysterious weapon known to no other warrior, not even his foster brother Fer Diad, who trained beside Cú Chulainn with Scáthach. Not just the women of Ulaid, but other ladies from exotic lands found him beautiful beyond all men, with his perfect body and his tri-colored hair caught in plaits down his back. When he prepared for combat and his warp-spasm transformed his body, he became even more attractive to them. Curious how ideas of beauty vary from place to place, isn't it?

This story began before Cú Chulainn wed Emer. We heard before how the Cú was on his way home from Alba after his training and stopped at the Isles, where he met a king's daughter and arranged a tryst with her. This is her sad story, for not all romances end well. No one from the Otherworld figures in this story, but the heroine, Derb Forgaill, was able to take bird shape, just like Cáer Ibormeith, Étaín, and other ladies of the *síd*.

The lesson in this tale is about men who ignored the wrath of the woman-troop when the ladies thought themselves betrayed.

Derb Forgaill, daughter of the king of Lochlann, fell in love with Cú Chulainn after hearing tales told of him. She came from the east with her handmaid. They flew in the shape of two geese bound together by a golden chain, aiming for Loch Cuan.

Where is Lochlann, you ask. Lochlann was Norway or Scotland or Germanic territories more generally, somewhere vaguely magical that lay north and east of Ériu. The Túatha Dé sailed from that direction to Eriu.

You might also ask: what kind of young women slip into goose suits and fly to Ériu in search of love? Derb Forgaill honored her tryst with the Cú.

Cú Chulainn was there by the side of the lake that day with his foster son Lugaid son of the Three Finds of Emain— the triplet sons of Eochu Feidlech by their sister Clothru. It was a troubled family history.

The two men caught sight of the birds.

"Bring down the birds," urged Lugaid.

Cú Chulainn let fly a shot with his sling that pierced the ribs of one bird and lodged in her womb. Suddenly, two human forms were before them on the strand.

"You are cruel to me," said the woman, "though I was seeking you."

"Too true," admitted Cú Chulainn.

He bent to suck the stone from the woman's side. It went into his mouth with a gulp of her blood.

"I swear, I came to seek you out," said she.

"It cannot be, girl," he said. "I cannot lie with a woman whose blood I have drunk."

She had come all that way. "Then give me to whomever you want."

"I think it good," said he, "that you should go to the lad who is the most noble in Ériu, Lugaib Riab nDerg." That was his fosterling Lugaid's nickname. He was called Three Stripes because he was marked by three red stripes on his body, although others argue that he was divided into three parts by bands of color in the skin at his waist and neck. Either way, incest never yields perfect fruit.

"That is acceptable," said she, "if I may continue to see you forever."

So she went to Lugaid and gave him a child.

One day at the end of winter, there was a great snow. The men at Emain made a giant pillar of snow. When the men were done fooling with it, the women climbed the pillar. They played a game.

"Let us piss on the pillar, to see whose urine will burn deepest. The woman who pisses right through the mound is clearly best at satisfying a man."

It all had to do with muscle control.

None of them could do it. They called for Derb Forgaill. She was not happy about it, for she was not a time-waster. Still, she climbed the pillar. Her piss shot from her through the pillar and into the earth.

The woman-troop huddled. "If the men find this out, no one will seem desirable compared to this woman. We should pluck out her eyes and cut off her nostrils and her ears and her plaits. She won't be so desirable then." They tortured her thus and then carried her to her house.

The men were in council on the hill at Emain.

"Strange, Lugaid," said Cú Chulainn, gazing toward the settlement, "there is snow on Derb Forgaill's house."

Snow on the roof. Hearth unlit. Wives always kept the hearth fire going during the day.

"Then she must be dying," cried Lugaid.

The two of them raced to the house. When Derb Forgaill heard them coming, though, she secured the door against them.

"Open up," shouted Cú Chulainn.

"Fair the bloom under which we parted," said she.

Then she went on:

Cú Chulainn bids me farewell,
The one I sought far from home,
And Lugaid, too, eager to have me,
The one whom I came to love.

But now I must travel afar
And my journey is not a happy one.
I am forced to part from both—
Unless death does not come for me.
With Cú Chulainn and with Lugaid,
Fear and terror were always at bay.
If it were not for blame and atonement,
Our union would not be a tragedy.
But a union with Riab nDerg destroyed,
It is a spike in the heart, blood of my breast.

Taken from Cú Chulainn forever,
A calamity if not for a fort-stone,
If not for the kingly stone of Lugaid's fort.
Every obstruction yields bloodshed.
Our joyful play was too brief
With the son of the Three Find Emmas.
That I will not see Cú Chulainn
Has made me tearfully morbid.
My tribe is landless, wretched with wailing
And parting from Lugaid.

My fian-comrade has not betrayed me—
Cú Chulainn, he loved boasting.
And my highborn, happy companion,
Lugaid mac Clothrann of Crúachan.
Gifted with manliness, with more skills than anyone,
Cú Chulainn, whose shapely body was famous.
A talent with weapons had lithe Lugaid,
And I was granted beauty above all women.

Still, every gift is lost in time,
Anyone may attract envy.
All treasure is useless in the grave,
Every strong man ends up woeful, wretched.
Every tryst in this world leads to longing,
Whatever you do, it won't lead to heaven.
A deadly tryst finished—beyond all riches—
A fair face, though lovely its complexion.
A hardened heart cannot be blessed.
It trusts a foreign tribe.
A face in the moment of misery
Changes and changes again.

When we used to drive around Emain,
There was never a bad adventure.
Cú Chulainn was happy then,
And Lugaid son of Clothru.
Cú Chulainn conversing with me,
With feats, with gifts,
But my heart grew whole
When I shared a bed with Lugaid.
We were torn from our play,
Though we might have been at it forever.
I doubt we shall meet again.
I am destined for death.

They say that she was not yet dead when the two men broke into the house. They say, too, that Lugaid dropped dead immediately upon seeing her. Then Cú Chulainn ran back to the house where the other women were hiding and razed it over them, so that neither man or woman was left alive in that house. Three fifties of queens, he killed them all.

Then Cú Chulainn lamented,

Derb Forgaill of the snow-white breast,
She sought me over the salty sea.
It was only a friendly favor she granted me,
The daughter of the king of all Lochlann.

From between two burial mounds
My wounded heart beats with sorrow.
Derb Forgaill's face under a stone on the slope,
Lugaid Ríab nDerg, alas for him.

Lugaid was of great renown,
He excelled at slaughtering.
What Lugaid chose
Was imposed upon Derb Forgaill.

Lugaid was of great renown,
Everyone knew that he was best.
He took fifty heads in battle
Before every full moon.

Derb Forgaill, famed for radiance,
For purity, and for modesty,
Her heart was never arrogant,
Her place was next to her husband.

Three fifties of women in Emain,
I brought slaughter upon them.
When the tribal kings gave judgment,
They knew the value of Derb Forgaill.

That is, Dér daughter of Forgall, king of Lochlainn.
Her grave was dug and her stone raised by Cú Chulainn.

A woman on her own in a place far from home, except for her handmaid. A husband she had not sought and the man she had wanted. No kin, no status but wife, no place but her house. Wives and daughters whose homeland she invaded were jealous of their men. The conflicts and triumphs of women wrecked lives and caused death, just as men did, but not usually on the pages of stories.

"The woman in the green cloak came to him smiling, but she raised a horsewhip and struck him."

THE NINTH TALE

Serglige Con Culainn—The Sick Bed of Cú Chulainn

IF *THE COURTSHIP OF ÉTAÍN* shows us that love can outlast life, and the tale of Derb Forgaill warns of passion's perils, this story is about the consequences of a successful courtship. It may seem like yet another amorous adventure of the dazzling Cú Chulainn, but the tale also asks questions about the hero. Can a real hero ever be true to one woman, or must he endlessly enthrall new women to maintain his reputation?

The Cú betrayed Emer time and again. Surely she could have found someone more loyal, if less epic, than Cú Chulainn to love. Other women who roamed medieval Irish literature managed to seek and attract men other than their husbands. Consider Medb, the queen and general of Connacht's armies—she was never without a bedmate. Or Scáthach and Aífe, who had children and lovers, but no husbands. Still, many medieval love stories end with nothing but a shallow promise or a woman's abandonment, or sometimes, dead bodies. This tale shows us what happens after a successful courtship: marriage.

There is a peculiar flaw in this story. One tradition—or one author—held that Cú Chulainn was married not to

Emer, but to a woman named Eithne in Gubai. The first half of this story treats Eithne as the wife who bickers with Cú Chulainn. Perhaps her name influenced the storyteller, or else the story itself granted her a name, for *guba* means sighing or lamenting. A different scholar finished the tale, though, or joined bits of several tales together, and put Emer back in command. It may be the worst insult of all to be so easily mixed up with another woman in a story. I tell the tale as I found it written, so that Eithne begins it and Emer ends it.

Another title for this story is "The Only Jealousy of Emer," which not only confirms that it is Emer's tale but also suggests her fortitude and the strength of her devotion to her husband. Cú Chulainn dallied with plenty of women, but his wife never objected until the events in this tale. Some scholars read Emer's dilemma as satirical, as if no one actually feared her anger. Perhaps they never heard the sad history of Derb Forgaill. If a woman-troop came for Emer, I wager that she could cut out their eyeballs. It is true, though, that this tale has plenty of humor as well as plenty of pain. Cú Chulainn was lucky to have such a wife as Emer, and lucky to live through this tale, all the way to the end.

Another thing about Emer: she would not permit an unhappy ending.

The Ulaid held an annual assembly that began three days before Samain and lasted until three days after. That is how long the Ulaid spent in Mag Muirthemne during the Samain assembly every year. Nothing got done in that time except games and gatherings, delights and diversions, feasting and feeding. Because of this ancient custom, we still observe the three stages of Samain throughout Ériu.

One time, the Ulaid were holding their assembly. Everyone used to gather to hear the warriors boast of their valor and triumphs at Samain. It was their custom to attend the assembly bringing the tongues of men they had killed tucked in their bags. Some cheaters added the tongues of cattle to increase their number. Each man would announce his triumphs in turn. They had to wear their swords at their thighs when they announced their triumphs, for the swords would turn against those who made false boasts.

Some tellers have suggested that the swords were inhabited by demons who called out liars. But, of course, there were no demons in Ériu before the Christians came.

That particular year, all the Ulaid had arrived at the assembly except two, namely, Conall Cernach and Fergus Mac Roich.

"Let the assembly begin," the Ulaid decreed.

"It will not begin until Conall and Fergus arrive," insisted Cú Chulainn. Fergus was his foster father and Conall his foster brother.

Sencha the druid said, "Why don't we play *fidchell* while we wait? Let the poets chant stories and bring on the jugglers." That is what they did.

They were still at it when a flock of birds alit on the lake nearby. There were no such spectacular birds anywhere in Ériu. The women were very eager to possess them. They began to argue about who might get a bird.

What they wanted them for, I leave to you. Let us say only that they did not need the birds alive.

Eithne Aiten Cháithrech, wife and queen of Conchobar, said, "I should like one bird upon each of my two shoulders."

"We all want that," chorused the women.

"If anyone gets a bird, it should be me first," cried Eithne in Gubai, wife of Cú Chulainn.

"What should we do?" asked the other women.

"Not difficult," said Leborcham the Seer, daughter of Óa and Adarc. "I shall ask Cú Chulainn."

So Leborcham went to Cú Chulainn and said, "The women want you to get them birds."

He grabbed his sword and shook it at her. He sneered, "The sluts of Ulaid want nothing except that we should hunt birds for them today?"

"That is rude," said Leborcham. "They will be angry, given that the third blemish to strike the women of Ulaid is your fault."

The women of Ulaid suffered three famous blemishes: crookedness, stammering, and half-blindness. Every woman who loved Conall Cernach had a crooked neck because Conall had a boil on his neck the size of a shield boss. Every woman who loved Cúscraid Mend Macha, son of Conchobar, used to stammer like he did. Likewise, every woman who loved Cú Chulainn made herself half-blind to resemble him while in his warrior's frenzy. When he became battle-mad, he sucked one eye so far into his head that even a crane could not pluck it out. The other eye he blew outward until it became the size of a cauldron big enough to boil a calf.

"Prepare the chariot for us, Lóeg," sighed Cú Chulainn.

Lóeg yoked the chariot. Cú Chulainn climbed into it and off they went. He launched a stunning strike at the birds, so that their claws and feathers floated on the water. He snagged them all then and brought them back so that they might be doled out to the women, and every woman had two birds except Eithne in Gubai, his own wife.

He approached his wife. "You are unhappy," he said to her.

"Not unhappy," said Eithne, "for I was the one who distributed them. It is fitting," said she. "There is not a woman among them who doesn't love you or would not share herself with you. I give my love only to you."

"Do not be unhappy then," said Cú Chulainn. "The day that birds come to Mag Muirthemne or the Bóinn, the two most beautiful birds will be yours."

It was not long after when they saw two birds upon the lake, linked with a red-gold chain. They sang a little and slumber fell over the host.

Cú Chulainn rose to go after them.

"Listen to me," said Eithne, "Do not chase them, for there is some power behind those birds. Other birds are fine for me."

"Is it at all likely that I would *not* go after them?" asked Cú Chulainn. "Lóeg, put a stone in my sling."

Lóeg found a stone and set it in the sling. Cú Chulainn let the stone fly. He missed.

He cursed and found another stone, but he overshot. "I'm a failure!" he said. "Ever since I first took up weapons, I have never missed a shot—until today."

Finally, he hurled his spear. It pierced the wing of one bird, but the two birds skimmed away over the water.

Cú Chulainn went after them. After a while, though, he decided to sit and rest with his back against a large stone. He fell asleep, still disgruntled.

He seemed to see two women coming toward him. One wore a green cloak, and the other had a five-fold crimson cloak around her. The woman in the green cloak came to him smiling, but she raised a horsewhip and struck him. The other one also approached smiling but began to beat him in the same way. They were at it for a long time, taking turns flogging him until he was almost dead. They left him there asleep.

The Ulaid found him. They debated whether to wake him. "Ach!" cried Fergus. "Do not disturb his dream-vision." Cú Chulainn finally awoke.

"Who did this to you?" they asked.

He could not speak. They carried him to bed. He spent a year lying there without speaking to anyone.

One day before the next Samain, some of the Ulaid were with him in the house. Fergus stood between him and the wall, Conall Cernach by the bedpost, Lugaid Riab nDerg by his pillow, and Eithne in Gubai was at his feet. As they stood there, an unfamiliar man appeared in the house and came to sit at the foot of Cú Chulainn's bed.

"What brings you here?" asked Conall Cernach.

"Not hard to tell," said he. "If this man were healthy, he would guarantee my safety among you. Even while he is sick and wounded, indeed, he remains an even greater guarantee that you will not harm me. I do not fear anyone here. I have come to confer with him."

"Welcome to you. Do not fear," said the curious Ulaid folk.

The man got up to recite these verses below:

> Cú Chulainn, who lies so still,
> Idling won't make you well.
> As allies, they could bring aid,
> The daughters of fair-eyed Áed.
>
> Said Lí Ban in Mag Crúach
> Standing with Labraid Lúathlám,
> "It is the heart's desire of Fand
> To sleep with Cú Chulainn."

[Fand:]   *"Joyful the day would be,*
if Cú Chulainn came to me.
Silver and gold he would gain,
And to drink, plenty of wine.

If he were my love, then,
Cú Chulainn, Súaldam's son,
He might tell me of his dream
If we were alone for a time."

[Óengus:]   *In Muirthemne, here in the south,*
Samain eve brings no threat.
If Lí Ban comes, you'll be well,
Cú Chulainn, who lies so still.

"Who are you?" they all asked the stranger.

"I am Óengus son of Áed Abrat." Then he left them, and they did not know where he might have gone nor whence he had come.

Cú Chulainn roused himself and spoke.

"Good timing," said the Ulaid. "Tell us what happened to you."

He said, "I saw a vision last year at Samain." He told them everything just as he had seen it—about the birds, the rock, the ferocious women. "What next, Papa Conchobar?" asked Cú Chulainn.

"What's next," said Conchobar, "is that you must return to the same stone."

What type of stone, I wonder, how large, how did it come there, what was it for? Like the massive boulders that formed tombs? Or the standing stones arranged in a circle that dotted Ériu? Or a carved boundary-marker. A grave marker.

Cú Chulainn walked back to the stone, where he saw the woman in the green cloak approaching.

"Well met, Cú Chulainn" said she.

"Not so well for me, I must say, was your visit last year," said wary Cú Chulainn.

"We have not come to harm you," said she, "but to seek your friendship. I wish to speak with you on behalf of Fand, daughter of Áed Abrat. Her husband, Manannán Mac Lir, has left her and thus she has decided to give all her love to you. I am Lí Ban and my husband, Labraid Lúathlám ar Claideb, has declared that he will give Fand to you in exchange for one day's combat against Senach Síaborthe and Echach Íuil and Éogan Indber."

Suspicious characters, those. Labraid's nickname was Swift Hand on a Sword. Senach's epithet means "ghostly" or "spectral." The other two are a secret of the *síd*.

"This is not a good day for me to fight," Cú Chulainn said.

"Your affliction will not last," said Lí Ban. "You will be well again and whatever power you lost will only increase. Labraid made that happen, for he is the greatest warrior in the world."

"Where is this place?" asked Cú Chulainn.

"Mag Mell," said the woman. "I must return there."

"Lóeg should go with you," said Cú Chulainn, "to have a look at your land."

"Let him come along, then," said Lí Ban.

Lí Ban and Lóeg went to find Fand.

Lí Ban caught Lóeg by the shoulder. "You should not leave here today," said Lí Ban, "unless you have a woman's protection."

"I'm not used to women's protection," said Lóeg.

"I wish it were Cú Chulainn here instead of you," complained Lí Ban.

"I would be happier if he were here," agreed Lóeg.

Still, they pushed on until they reached a lake and, in its middle, an island. They watched as a bronze boat crossed the lake toward them. They climbed into the boat and crossed to the island. There they found a house where a man met them at the door.

It was not the same door, same man, house, island, or boat that Becfola found. More than one *síd* happened to be on an island.

Then Lí Ban said,

Where is Labraid Lúathlám ar Claideb
Who leads the triumphant troops,
Victorious in a charging chariot,
He with the blood-soaked spear-points?

The man answered her:

Labraid is fierce and vicious,
Never slow, his men are numerous.
His warbands will bring slaughter
To Mag Fidgae, full of attackers.

They entered the house after that and saw three fifties of couches with three fifties of women lounging on them. All the women saluted Lóeg. This is what they said to him: "Welcome, Lóeg, for the sake of the one who came with you, the one who sent you, and for your own sake."

"What will you do now, Lóeg?" asked Lí Ban. "Shall you go to speak with Fand?"

"I shall, if I know where."

"In a private chamber."

They went then to speak to her. She welcomed them in the same manner. Fand was the daughter of Áed Abrat, which means "fiery eyelash." The pupil in the iris is the fire of the eye. Fand's name means the tear that veils the eye. She was named after a teardrop because of her purity and beauty, for she had no equal in the world.

While convening there, they heard the sound of an approaching chariot. Labraid was coming.

"Labraid is angry today," said Lí Ban. "We must go and speak to him."

They went out. Lí Ban welcomed him, saying,

Welcome, Labraid Lúathlám ar Claideb!
Heir of troops
Of swift spearmen,
He sunders shields,
He scatters spears
He bloodies bodies,
He wastes warlords,
Seeks slaughter—
Lovelier than ladies—
He annihilates armies,
He tosses treasures.
Wrecker of warriors, welcome!
Welcome, Labraid.

Labraid did not answer so the maiden said,

Welcome Labraid Lúathlám ar Claideb of battle!
Ready with favors,
Generous to all,

Eager for fighting,
Battle-scarred body,
Honest his word,
Protector of right,
Friendly his rule,
Daring his sword hand,
Vengeful, valorous,
He cuts down champions.
Welcome, Labraid!

Labraid still did not respond, so she sang yet another verse:

Welcome Labraid Lúathlám ar Claideb!
More manly than boys,
Bolder than chieftains,
He crushes the brave,
Battles battalions,
Slashes young fighters,
Fires up the weak,
And wastes the mighty.
Welcome Labraid Lúathlám ar Claideb!

"What you say is not right, woman," said Labraid, and then he sang:

I am not arrogant or aloof, woman,
Nor do I prefer pride over prudence.
We face a struggle surrounded by spear-points,
Our rights hand brandishing bloody blades,
Against the fanatical forces of Eochaid Íuil.
I have no haughtiness.
I am not arrogant or aloof, woman.

"Cheer up," said Lí Ban. "Here is Lóeg, charioteer of Cú Chulainn, with the message that he will bring a host."

Labraid greeted him. "Welcome Lóeg, for the sake of the woman with whom you came and everyone who sent you. Go home now, Lóeg. Lí Ban will follow you."

Lóeg returned to Emain and told his story to Cú Chulainn and everyone else. Cú Chulainn sat up and passed a hand over his face. Then he spoke clearly with Lóeg. The news brought home by his charioteer raised his spirits.

And as for Eithne . . .

There was an assembly of the four provinces of Ériu at that time, to decide whether they could choose someone to be king of all Ériu. For they thought it wrong that the capital of the lordship and chieftaincy of Ériu, that is, Temair, should lack a rightful king; and wrong that the tribes should live together without the judgment of a king. For the men of Ériu had been without royal judgement for seven years after the destruction of the previous king Conaire in the hall of Dá Derga, until the great assembly of four provinces of Ériu at Temair in the house of Erc son of Cairpre Nia Fer. Conaire had made so many mistakes and broken so many of his *gessa* that his rule ended in death and conflagration.

Erc Mac Coirpri was the grandson of Conchobar. He was another intemperate king with a special animus against Cú Chulainn. That tale was yet to happen when Cú Chulainn was still in his sickbed.

So the provincial kings gathered, that is, Medb and Ailill, Cú Roí, Tigernach Tétbannach mac Luchtai, and Finn mac Rossa. They did not allow the Ulaid to take part in the council because all the other provinces were allied against the northerners. That, too, was a tale yet to come.

They carried out the Bull-feast to discover who should receive the kingship. A white bull was slaughtered. One man had his fill of the meat and its broth. He fell asleep while sated, and four druids sang a spell of truth over him. In his dream he saw the sort of man who should be made king, based on his appearance, his behavior, and the kind of job he would do. The dreamer awakened from his trance and told his dream to the tribal kings, that is, his vision of a strong young noble warrior with two red stripes on him. This warrior was then standing by the pillow of the man with wasting-sickness in Emain Macha.

Messengers were sent to Emain. At that time, the Ulaid were assembled around Conchobar while Cú Chulainn was in his sickbed there. They told their news to Conchobar and the noblemen of Ulaid.

"With us now is the son of a noble lineage with just those qualifications," said Conchobar, "namely Lugaid Riab nDerg, son of the Three Finds of Emain, foster son of Cú Chulainn. He is by the Cú's pillow right over there, entertaining his foster father, Cú Chulainn, who is sick."

One small issue: Lugaid had three stripes in the previous story, not two.

Cú Chulainn sat up then to give his foster son some advice:

> *The Precepts of Wisdom of Cú Chulainn*
> *Do not incite coarse, combative conflict.*
> *Be not brazen, bellicose, boorish.*
> *Be not hesitant, harsh, hasty, hotheaded.*
> *Do not descend into drunken degeneracy.*

Be not the annoying flea at the king's ale-feasts.
Be not the man who malingers in the marches.
Do not dally with disreputable dependents.

Do not limit legal claims because of little details.
Let memories advise as to heirs of the soil.
Let learned men discuss propriety in your presence.
Let law-keepers consider kinship and property.
Let lineages lengthen with each new babe.
Let the living be summoned, the dead recalled
*   by their oaths to the places they ploughed.*
Let heirs be maintained on their lawful legacies.
Let outsiders go forth with proper protection.

Do not argue on,
Do not speak noisily.
Do not play a fool,
Do not call another man fool.
Do not browbeat the old ones,
Do not be unfriendly.
Do not ask the impossible.
Do not deny a man without cause.
Lend well. Grant fairly. Pledge well.

Be humbly instructed by the wise.
Be polite when guided by elders.
Be mindful of ancestral ways.
Be not cold to your friends.
Be on fire toward your enemies.
Be not contentious in councils.
Be not loud and loquacious.
Do not bully.

Do not hoard for no profit.
Restrain from reproving righteous behavior.
Do not stomp on your scruples to please someone.
Do not lash out lest you regret it.
Be not abusive lest you turn evil.
Be not lazy lest you languish.
Be not too eager lest you be vulgar.
Adhere to these words, my son!

Then Lugaid said to Cú Chulainn:

For the good of all,
Every man should know it,
For nothing is lacking from it,
And it shall be handed down as is.

Lugaid went then to the halls at Temair and was proclaimed king, and the Feast of Temair was celebrated that night, after which everyone went home.

Now, some storytellers maintain that this episode about Lugaid and the Bull-feast merely interrupts the tale of Cú Chulainn's illness. After all, what did the hero know about kingship? He was never king of anything. He was certainly not prudent, nor was he much given to reflection about truth and righteousness, let alone legal niceties. Still, he was fond of his foster son and Lugaid Riab nDerg did require guidance—for instance, when he tried to marry Cú Chulainn's betrothed.

As for Cú Chulainn, let us continue with the tale. Or perhaps we are entering a different tale, because the hero seems to have a more familiar wife, a stronger wife, a wife who will not serenely stand by while a woman from the *síd* sickens and summons her heedless husband.

"Go now to Emer, Lóeg" said Cú Chulainn, "and tell her that women of the *síd* came to me and destroyed me, and that I am recuperating, and she should come to visit me."

The charioteer answered Cú Chulainn:

> *What great folly for a warrior*
> *To lie half-asleep in his sickbed.*
> *It proves that sprites*
> *From the folk of Tenmag Trogaige*
> *Could abuse you*
> *Bind you,*
> *Torture you,*
> *Through the power of womanly lust.*
> *Arise from the banshee's spell!*
> *Your martial skills will flourish*
> *Among champions and fighters.*
> *Be hale and whole,*
> *Be done with it,*
> *Do great deeds.*
> *When Labraid cries out for help,*
> *O red-blooded warrior,*
> *Rise up so that you may be great again!*

Still, the charioteer went to Emer and repeated what Cú Chulainn told him to say.

"Shame on you, charioteer," said she, "for you visited the *síd* and returned without a cure for your lord. Woe to the Ulaid," said she, "for not seeking to heal him. If Conchobar were consumed, or Fergus felled, or Conall Cernach worse for wounds, Cú Chulainn would care for them."

Then she sang a lay:

Alas, son of Ríangabar,
Though you walked among the Other,
You did not rush home with a cure
For the son of Deichtine's nightmare.

Shame upon Ulaid, full of care
For foster fathers and foster brothers,
But not searching mortal lands
To aid their darling Cú Chulainn.

If Fergus had fallen to spells
That a famous druid might dispel,
The son of Deichtine would not rest
Until the curse was reversed.

And if it were Conall Cernach
Tortured by wounds and aches,
The Cú would search everywhere
To bring Conall a doctor's care.

If it were Lóegaire Búadach
Whom danger ruined and wracked,
He would search all of Ériu's plains
To heal Connad Mac Ilíach's son.

If it were Celtchar, famously sly,
Who suffered the sleeping malady,
Sétanta would rove for days until
He had scoured the Hollow Hills.

If Furbaide the Fían warrior
Was waiting to recover,
The Cú would roam the solid earth
Till Furbaide's health returned.

The troops of Síd Truim are crushed,
Their great deeds are dispersed,
Their Cú does not outrace the pack
Since a síd-dream made him weak.

Your illness takes my breath,
Hound of Conchobar's smith,
My heart and soul are troubled
Trying to finish this struggle.

Alas, my heart's own blood,
The horseman lies pale in his bed
Until he returns, healed and hale,
Home from Muirthemne's council.

From Emain he cannot come,
We're divided by a phantom.
My voice grows thin and fades,
While he lies in a shameful state.

A month, a season, a year
Since we two have slept together,
Since I heard my love's sweet words,
O son of Ríangabar.

Then Emer traveled to Emain to visit Cú Chulainn. She sat on his bed and scolded him, "Shame on you, lying around for of love for a woman. If you just lie there, you will become truly ill." And then she chanted:

> *Rise up, warrior of Ulaid!*
> *Awakened, cured, contented!*
> *The ruler of Emain rises early,*
> *You must not linger in lethargy.*

> *See his shoulder, glittering with gems,*
> *See his splendid drinking horns,*
> *See the chariots that charge through the glens,*
> *See the fighters on his fidchell board,*

> *See his heroes, a hardy force,*
> *See his tall and lithesome ladies,*
> *See his kings—a combative course—*
> *See the gentle queens of his court.*

> *See the sparkle of winter's start,*
> *See each wonder in its turn,*
> *See around you now, what you serve:*
> *World frozen forever, an endless eve.*

> *Heavy sleep squeezes life from your limbs,*
> *Your rest results from oppression within,*
> *Like another drop in an over-full pail*
> *The frailer you are, the sooner you fail.*

> *Rise from sleep, from spell-drunken dolor,*
> *Fling it away with passionate force,*
> *You are washed in many loving words,*
> *Rise up, warrior of Ulaid!*

Cú Chulainn started up then and passed a hand over his face. He threw off his weariness and the weight of his dreams. He rose up and came away to Airbe Rofír in Conaille Murthemne. There he saw Lí Ban approaching. The woman spoke to him and invited him into the *síd*.

"Where is Labraid?" asked Cú Chulainn.

"Not hard," said she.

Labraid dwells by a cool, clear lake
Where women visit for his sake.
It won't be hard to reach that place
And let King Labraid make his case.

A hundred fall with one hand's blow,
As the one who tells you knows—
A scarlet flower blooms in each
Of Labraid Lúath's lovely cheeks.

Conchend, keen for battle, shakes
Before Labraid's slender bloodied blade.
He breaks the spears of frenzied bands
And smashes shields from hostile hands.

In combat, eyes and face agleam,
He never fails his friends in need,
Nobler than most men of the mounds,
The man who has slaughtered thousands.

More renowned than younger men
He invaded Eochaid Íuil's lands.
With hair as fine as golden threads,
The scent of wine perfumes his breath.

Best of men, he's first to fight,
He keeps his kingdom's boundaries tight,
Wind-borne boats and galloping steeds
Race past the island where Labraid abides.

A man of triumphs overseas,
Labraid Lúathlam ar Claideb,
No skirmishing disturbs his peace
His multitudes enjoy their sleep.

Red gold bridles tame his herds,
Nothing more can be put in words:
Pillars of silver and crystal rise,
This is the house where he abides.

"I won't go at the invitation of a woman," said Cú Chulainn.

"Let Lóeg come along then," said the woman, "and see it all."

"Let him go then," said Cú Chulainn.

Lóeg went with the maiden then to Mag Lúada, and the Bile Búada, and past the Óenach nEmna and Óenach Fidgai, and found Áed Abrat with his daughters. Fand welcomed Lóeg.

"Why did Cú Chulainn not come?" asked she.

That is the crucial question. After all, it was the second time that Lóeg took his place.

"He did not care to come at a woman's invitation, not until he made sure that it came from you."

"It was from me," said she, "so fetch him quickly, for the battle takes place today."

Lóeg returned immediately to Cú Chulainn.

"How is it, Lóeg?" asked Cú Chulainn.

Lóeg answered, "We must go at once," said he, "because the battle will take place today."

And thus he sang a lay:

I arrived to find splendid play,
A place both strange and familiar to my eye,
I found a cairn and scores of companies,
Where long-haired Labraid abides.

I found him at the mound
Sitting, with weapons all around,
His hair is yellow, a glittering tint,
And an apple of gold clasping it.

He recognized me, I expect,
By my five-folded crimson cloak.
He said, "Will you accompany me then
to the house wherein is Fáilbe Find?"

There are two kings in the abode,
Fáilbe Find and Labraid,
Three fifties around each of the two
Is the number in their retinues.

Fifty beds on the right side,
And fifty on the floor,
Fifty couches on the left side,
And on the platform fifty more.

Bedpost of bronze there
And bright gilded pillars

The seeming candle that shone
Is a precious bright stone.

Before the western door, which lets
The sun shine in as it sets,
Is a herd of grey horses with spotted manes
Another herd is chestnut brown.

Through the eastward portal
Stand three trees of purple crystal,
The constant twitter of a flock of birds
Sings for the children in the royal fort.

There is a tree at the entrance gate,
Its harmony a true delight,
A silver post upon which the sun shines,
Turning to gold its brilliance.

Three twenties of trees rise
Whose crowns intertwine beneath the skies.
Mast to feed three hundred men
Comes from every branch of them.

In the síd there is also a certain well,
Where lie three fifties of bright-dyed mantles,
And on each one a brooch of gold
To clasp the mantles' many folds.

There's a cauldron full of quality mead
Doled out to meet each warrior's need,
It was always there and is there still,
For that cauldron is always foaming full.

There is a maiden in the house, too,
Who could outshine the women of all Ériu.
Her golden hair flows all around,
Her beauty and charm bring her renown.

The conversation she carries on
Is intoxicating to everyone.
She breaks more hearts than any one
Because they love her, down to a man.

The maiden said then
"Who is the unfamiliar one?
If it be you, come closer to me,
Servant of the man of Muirthemne."

I approached her most cautiously,
As fear for my honor seized me
But she asked me only, "Will he come,
Delightful Deichtine's only son?"

Too bad that he himself did not come,
For everyone else there seeks him,
He could view for himself if he dared,
The marvelous house that I saw there.

If I should rule all Ériu
The kingship of gracious Brega, too,
I would throw it away, I promise you,
To live in that place I was led to.

"That sounds good," said Cú Chulainn.

"It is good," agreed Lóeg. "And it is proper to go to her, for everything in that land is wonderful."

Lóeg continued reciting the pleasures of the *síd.*

I saw a bright noble stronghold
Where lies and untruths are never told.
There rules a king who sheds men's blood,
Labraid Lúathalm ar Claideb.

Going across Mag Lúada
I was shown Bile Búada.
In Mag Denna I managed to take
A pair of strange two-headed snakes.

It was then that Lí Ban said
Approaching the place where we were sent,
"It would be a wonder, indeed,
If the Cú were here in your stead."

Lovely woman-troop—triumph without limit—
The daughters of Áed Abrat,
The shapely Fand—sound so bright—
Neither queen nor king can compete.

I could list, as I have found,
The descendants of Adam without sin,
Yet such is the beauty of Fand
That of her like, there is none.

I saw gleaming men of war,
Slashing with their swords,

I saw them in colorful array,
Their raiment was not lowly.

I saw gentlewomen at a feast
I saw their daughters next.
I saw young men of privilege
Wandering the wooded ridge.

In the house, I saw musicians
Playing for the maidens.
If I had not quickly fled
I, too, would be put in sick bed.

I saw the hill where she was sitting,
Eithne in Gubai, her name is fitting,
But the woman sung of in these lines
Could drive men from their minds.

Oh, dear. There is Eithne again. I meant Emer.

Cú Chulainn went afterward into that land. By chariot they reached the island. Labraid welcomed him and so did the whole woman-troop. Fand gave a special welcome to Cú Chulainn.

"What must be done?" asked Cú Chulainn.

"Not hard," said Labraid. "We must go first and estimate the size of the host."

They went out then and spotted the massed enemy troops. They cast an eye over them, and the host was innumerable.

"Go from here now," said Cú Chulainn to Labraid.

Labraid left Cú Chulainn facing the enemy army alone.

Two druidical ravens warned the army of his presence. The fighters noticed the birds and they all said, "The ravens are telling us that the Warped One of Ériu is here." The armies hunted the ravens until there was no safe place for the birds in the territory.

Eochaid Íuil came early that morning to wash his hands at the spring. Cú Chulainn sighted Eochaid's shoulder through his cloak and hurled his spear at the target.

That was just the beginning. All by himself, he killed thirty-three warriors. Senach Síaborthe attacked him and fought fiercely until Cú Chulainn killed him, too.

Labraid arrived then with his men and routed the armies. He asked for a halt to the slaughter.

Lóeg warned, "The Warped One may turn his anger on us, for the battle did not offer enough fighting to satisfy him. Best to go and prepare three vats of cold water to extinguish his fury."

When Cú Chulainn jumped into the first vat, the water boiled around him. When he entered the second, it grew so hot that others could not touch it. When he went into the third, it remained comfortably warm to the touch.

When the women saw Cú Chulainn, this is what Fand sang:

Stately the chariot-fighter that travels the road
Though the beardless warrior be not old;
Lovely the driver who crosses the way
At evening, after Óenach Fidgai.

The music of the síd is not his song,
Blood stains him as he rumbles along
And the humming that comes with him
Is the tune his chariot wheels sing.

The horses yoked to his steady chariot,
If only they paused so I could have a look,
A pair like them cannot be found,
They are as swift as a spring wind.

Fifty golden baubles he plays with,
Lifting them up with his breath:
Among kings there is no man like him,
Among the kind or among the grim.

In each of his cheeks you shall find
A shade of red like fresh blood,
A shade of green, a shade of blue,
And a shade of lightest purple, too.

Seven pupils are in each eye—
No chance of leaving him blind!
An ornament of his noble view
Are his lashes of black-blue.

His fame has already spread,
This young beardless lad,
It is told across the borders
That his hair is of many colors.

A bloody sword that grows redder still,
Up to its shining silver hilt,
A shield with a golden boss on,
Rimmed all around with white bronze.

He leaps over men in every duel,
He charges wherever there's peril:

Among your fiercest warrior bands
There is none like Cú Chulainn.

Cú Chulainn who came hither
The young warrior of Muirthemne,
To this place he was brought
By the daughters of Áed Abrat.

A long red drop of blood,
His flame rises tall as treetops.
His proud victory cry invokes
Dismal woe falling on síd folk.

Lí Ban greeted him then and said:

Welcome Cú Chulainn,
Bellicose boar,
The champion chief of Muirthemne,
His spirit is strong,
With the valor of a victor,
Heart of heroes,
Strong stone of wisdom,
Blood-red in rage,
Ready for fair fight,
Fierce flame of the Ulaid.
Lovely his light,
Lively eye for ladies,
He is welcome.
Welcome, Cú Chulainn.

"What have you done, Cú Chulainn?" Lí Ban asked him.

Cú Chulainn sang:

I loosed my spear
Into the camp of Éogan Inber,
I did not know, famous the way,
Whether I missed or gained the day.

Whether better or worse I fare,
I have never thrown before
A fair shot unknowingly into a mist.
Perhaps it left no man alive.

A brilliant fair host on choice steeds
Pursued me on all sides,
The troop of Manannán mac Lir
Was summoned by Éogan Inber.

I spun around all ways
When my full fury finally blazed,
It was one man against three thousand—
I cut every one of them down.

I heard the groan of Eochaid Íuil
Speaking from his heart and soul:
If by one, not an army, came ruin,
Then my aim was true.

Cú Chulainn slept with Fand and stayed a month in her company. As he bade her farewell at the end of the month, she asked, "Where shall we meet to tryst again?" They arranged to meet at Ibar Cind Tráchta in Ulaid territory.

Waiting at home, Emer learned everything. She immediately prepared knives with which to kill the woman. She came with fifty armed women to that tryst at Ibar Cind Tráchta.

As the women approached quietly, Cú Chulainn and Lóeg were playing *fidchell*. At first, they did not perceive the women creeping up on them. Fand must have been in the little house that Cú Chulainn had built for them.

But Fand saw the women and cried to Lóeg, "Look at what I see."

"What is it?" Lóeg asked. He looked around.

Fand, said, "Look, Lóeg, behind you. A troop of clear-minded, righteous women is listening to you, with sharpened knives gripped in their right hands and gold upon their breasts. Wait until these warriors climb into their battle chariots: Emer ingen Forgaill is about to change shape."

Into what? Did she, too, fall into frenzies? Or did she become manly when she wielded her weapon?

"Do not fear," said Cú Chulainn. "She will not get close enough. Climb into my powerful chariot with the sunny seat. I will save you from the women of the four quarters of Ulaid. Although the daughter of Forgall boasts to her co-fosterlings about her daring deeds, she will not challenge me."

Cú Chulainn then turned to face Emer. "I will dodge you, woman, as each man would avoid his angry loved one. I shall not strike down your trembling spear, nor your thin feeble knife, nor return your weak, limited anger, for my power is too devastating to unleash upon a woman's pitiful strength."

"A question then," demanded Emer. "Why did you dishonor me before all the women of our province, and indeed, of all Ériu, and before all the nobility besides? I came under your guarantee and mighty protection. Although you brag about your amazing war experiences, you cannot abandon me, lad, though you would try."

"A question for you, Emer," retorted Cú Chulainn, "Why can't you leave me be while I am trysting with a woman? For she is pure, modest, bright, clever, lovely, and worthy of a king. She is a truly handsome sight on the waves of the high-tided sea, with her shapeliness, attractive appearance, noble birth, and with her excellent needlework and handiwork and housework; with her sense and prudence and steadiness, with her abundance of horses and herds of cattle. There is nothing under heaven that she would not do if her husband asked her. And, Emer," he said, "You will never find a finer, battle-scarred, triumphant hero than me."

"Perhaps," said Emer bitterly, "this woman that you want is no better than me. I know, everything red is pretty, everything new is shiny, everything tall is attractive, everything familiar is stale. The untried is admirable, the well-known neglected, until everything new is old news. O lad," she moaned, "once you esteemed me, and it could be that way again, if I still pleased you."

Melancholy drenched him to the bones. "I swear, truly," said he, "you are dear to me, and you shall be as long as you live."

"You should leave me," interrupted Fand from the chariot.

"It is better that he leaves me," said Emer.

"Not so," said Fand. "I should be left behind, for I was threatened by your women a little while ago." She began to weep and lament at the shame of abandonment. She rushed into the little house. Her love for Cú Chulainn tortured her. She keened this poem:

> I will journey onward,
> Though I had high hopes here.
> Whoever might approach me, though great his fame,
> I would rather remain.

It's here I would rather be—
I admit it willingly,
though you may be surprised at that—
than back in the bower of Áed Abrat.

O Emer, the man is yours,
You should enjoy him, my good girl,
Although I cannot catch him,
I still want him.

Many men have sought me,
Both in public and in secrecy,
But I did not meet them anywhere
Because I valued my honor.

Woeful the woman who gives her heart
To one who does not care.
Better to deny her ardor
If she is not desired as she desires.

Fifty women arrived here
O Golden-haired Emer,
To ambush fair Fand—don't dare
To kill her in her despair.

Still, there are three fifties
Of women, lovely young ladies,
At home in my fort with me,
Who would never leave me.

At that point, Manannán Mac Lir, king of the sea, heard that Fand, daughter of Áed Abrat, was outnumbered and threatened by the women of Ulaid and that she was

abandoned by Cú Chulainn. Manannán came westward to
find her and stood before her, though no one could see him
except Fand. Regret and sadness overwhelmed her as she
gazed upon Manannán, and she made this poem:

> See the soldierly son of Ler
> Upon the plains of Éogan Inber:
> Manannán, ruling the world,
> Who used to be my beloved.

> Though today my heart is heavy,
> My proud mind is not in love,
> For love is a useless thing,
> Heedlessly skittering.

> When I was with Mac Lir
> In the bower of Dún Inbir,
> It seemed certain to us
> That nothing could separate us.

> When handsome Manannán married me
> I was a wifely ally.
> Back then he would always yield
> In our games of fidchell.

> When handsome Manannán married me,
> I behaved in a manner quite wifely.
> He bestowed on me a bracelet of gold
> As the price of my maidenhood.

> I had on the heath beyond
> Fifty lovely-complexioned women;

I brought fifty men to him
To be the women's companions.

Four fifties, not false,
Were the people of our house
Two fifties of hearty, thriving men
And two fifties of fair, fit women.

I saw on the ocean distant
—if you cannot, you are not blind—
A horseman upon the sea foam:
He did not need a ship to come home.

You rode on past us till now
Invisible to all but síd-folk.
You can make out an unseen company
However far off it may be.

That sight would be useful to me,
For women's perception is faulty;
He whom I loved so distractedly
Has left me here in jeopardy.

Farewell, darling Cú.
In peace we leave you.
I do not wish to go, though.
Every rule is right until broken.

It is time for me to depart—
Someone here finds that difficult,
For my distress grows ever greater,
O Loég, o son of Ríangabar.

I will go with my husband
For he will not leave me behind.
Where I go in secret you cannot say
Even if you look my way.

Fand went to Manannán then. He greeted her. "Well, wife, are you staying with Cú Chulainn or will you go with me?"

"Upon my word," said she, "there could be nothing better than being his wife. But," said she, "it is with you I shall go, and I shall not wait for Cú Chulainn, for he abandoned me. And there is another thing, my good man, you have no proper queen, but Cú Chulainn does."

When Cú Chulainn saw the woman leaving him with Manannán, he said to Lóeg, "What is going on?"

"Not hard," said Lóeg, "Fand is going with Manannán Mac Lir because she thinks she does not please you."

That's when Cú Chulainn made three high leaps and three southward leaps toward Lúachair. He spent a long time in the mountains without drinking or eating, and he slept every night on Slige Midlúachra.

Emer hurried to Conchobar in Emain and told him of Cú Chulainn's sorry state. Conchobor sent wise men and poets and druids of Ulaid to find him and bring him back to Emain. The Cú tried to kill the poets, but druids sang spells to weaken him so that they could bind him by the hands and feet until he came to his senses.

He asked them for drink. The druids brought a drink of forgetting to him and he downed it. He lost all memory of Fand and of what he had done. They also brought a drink of forgetting to Emer, who was in no better shape, so that she might lose her jealousy.

Manannán shook a cloak between Cú Chulainn and Fand so that they should never meet again.

Was it the right thing for the druids to do, relieving Cú Chulainn of his guilty desire and Emer of her anger? What about everyone else, did they keep the secret? Did the forty-nine women of Emer's band never whisper to her of betrayal? Did they ever take up their knives to teach a lesson to other men who strayed?

Everything new is shiny until somebody gets hurt. Cú Chulainn was led into secret pleasures by his Otherworldly woman, suffered her loss, and forgot her. Fand sadly returned to the king who once loved her. Emer regained her hero at the price of her memory. You might think that humans would learn not to mess with folk from the *síd*. Some medieval priests preached that the people of the Hollow Hills were all demons who took tempting forms precisely to mislead mortals to their doom. Other learned men of the distant past theorized that the folk of the *síd* were fallen angels who had remained neutral during Lucifer's rebellion. They were cast to earth but not sent to hell with the malicious angels, and the pagans of ancient times mistook them for gods. They can never enter the Christian heaven. The *síd* seems pretty close to it, though.

Most people in early medieval Ireland probably just shrugged and enjoyed the tales without worrying about whether *síd* souls could be saved. (There is one story, called "The Fosterage of the House of Two Milk Buckets," about a girl from the Túatha Dé who gave up her magic for baptism. It's not so old and you will not find it here.) I expect they kept an eye on local mounds and avoided certain caves and uncanny trees. They stayed snug in a clean house with a well-tended hearth fire on the eve of Samain. Some went to church on Sundays. The scribes who wrote these astonishing stories probably lived next door to churches. Like us, the people of the past could believe in more than one reality.

On one page of a twelfth-century Irish manuscript now called *Lebor Laigen* (Book of Leinster) are two epigraphs that assess some of the tales I have told here. A scribe who had just finished copying the *Táin Bó Cúailnge* added something in his native tongue:

> *Endacht ar cech óen mebraigfes go hindraic Táin amlaid seo 7 ná tuillfe cruth aile furri.*

> "A blessing on everyone who will repeat the Táin exactly as it is here and will not revise it."

Then along came another scribe, who wrote in Latin:

> *Sed ego qui scripsi hanc historiam aut uerius fabulam quibusdam fidem in hac historia aut fabula non accommodo. Quaedam enim ibi sunt praestrigia demonum, quaedam autem figmenta poetica, quaedam similia uero, quaedam non, quaedam ad delectationem stultorum.*

> "But I who have written this story, or rather fantasy, do not hold with certain episodes in it. For some episodes relate the tricks of demons, while others are poetical figments; some seem true, others not; while still others are for the amusement of fools."

The first writer was either an idealist or a dupe, because no one can tell a story without changing it. The second writer was a prim critic using the language of Christianity, but he had a sense of humor—for what is a story but deceptions and figments, which may or may not seem possible and true? Since he worked in two languages, the critic also knew that every storyteller is a translator who renders action into words, beliefs into plots and characters, vision into description, the past into the present, and sometimes one tongue into another.

The teller shapes the tale and the tale returns the favor, over and over again. Everyone is a fool for an amusing story of love and wonder.

AFTERWORDS

I MUST OFFER MORE THAN one word after retelling these tales. First, a word of thanks to a few helpers. Maria Tymoczko taught me my first words of Irish and encouraged me to pursue my studies in Ireland. For that I thanked and cursed her almost daily while working on these retellings. Deirdre Mullane believed that new versions of old stories could make a book that delights and also sells, for which I am grateful. I hope she is right. Likewise, editors and readers of Oxford University Press are taking a chance on yet another slim volume of revised medieval literature, but at least this one includes lots of sex, blood, and nice pictures. Nick, worthy hero, edited a draft. The inspiration for this volume came from Peter Mancall. He dreamed it up one day when we were living in rainy, dreary Oxford, in order to cheer me up and give me something to do. Like a man from the Otherworld, he brought me light, life, and love. Also an idea for a book.

Following is a list of some, though not all, previous translations and editions of the Irish texts in this volume, organized by story. In addition, I suggest where to find basic bibliographies of medieval Irish literature and the scholarship written about it, databases of digitized manuscripts, and other handy resources, should you want to study one or two of the tales. Finally, I offer a few suggestions for additional reading about the tales and the world from which they came. Be wary, though—if you venture into the territory of Óengus and Étaín, Cú Chulainn and Emer and Fand, you might not find your way out again. It happened to me.

As I mentioned before, this is not meant to be a comprehensive critical bibliography. For that, you must ask another scholar.

TRANSLATIONS AND EDITIONS

FOLLOWING ARE SOME EDITIONS AND translations of the stories that I consulted in comparison to my own translations. Many of these texts can be found in digital versions in the databases listed here as well.

Echtrae Chonnlae

McCone, Kim, ed. and trans. *Echtrae Chonnlai and the Beginnings of Vernacular Narrative Writing in Ireland.* Maynooth Medieval Irish Texts 1. Maynooth: Department of Old and Middle Irish, National University of Ireland, 2000.

Oskamp, Hans P. A. "Echtra Condla." *Études Celtiques* 14:1 (1974–1975): 207–228.

Tochmarc Étaíne

Bergin, Osborn, and R. I. Best, ed. and trans. "Tochmarc Étaíne." *Ériu* 12 (1934–1938): 137–196.

Carey, John, trans. ["Various Contributions."] In *The Celtic Heroic Age: Literary Sources for Ancient Celtic Europe and Early Ireland and Wales* (4th ed.), edited by John T. Koch and John Carey. Aberystwyth: Celtic Studies Publications, 2003. ($70.)

Gantz, Jeffrey, trans. *Early Irish Myths and Sagas.* Harmondsworth: Penguin, 1981: 37–59.

Aislinge Óenguso
Gantz, Jeffrey, trans. *Early Irish Myths and Sagas.* Harmondsworth: Penguin, 1981: 107–112.

Kelly, Patricia, ed. "Aislinge Oengusai." In *TLH: Thesaurus Linguae Hibernicae* (online): University College Dublin, 2006–2011. http://www.ucd.ie/tlh/text/pk.tlh.002.text.html. Accessed June 28, 2023.

Meid, Wolfgang, ed. and trans. *Die Suche nach der Traumfrau. Aislinge Óenguso: Oengus' Traum. Eine altirische Sage.* Innsbrucker Beiträge zur Kulturwissenschaft, Neue Folge, 14. Innsbruck: Institut für Sprachen und Literaturen der Universität Innsbruck, 2017.

Shaw, Francis, ed. *The Dream of Óengus: Aislinge Óenguso.* Dublin: Browne and Nolan, 1934.

Tochmarc Becfhola
Bhreathnach, Máire, ed. and trans. "A New Edition of Tochmarc Becfhola." *Ériu* 35 (1984): 59–91.

Dillon, Myles, ed. "The Wooing of Becfhola and the Stories of Cano, Son of Gartnán." *Modern Philology* 43:1—*Studies in Honor of Tom Peete Cross* (August 1945): 11–17.

Echtra Nerai
Carey, John, trans. ["Various Contributions."] In *The Celtic Heroic Age: Literary Sources for Ancient Celtic Europe and Early Ireland and Wales* (4th ed.), edited by John T. Koch and John Carey. Aberystwyth: Celtic Studies Publications, 2003 (§ 83).

Meyer, Kuno, ed. and trans. "The Adventures of Nera." *Revue Celtique* 10 (1889): 212–228, 520. Corrigenda in *Revue Celtique* 17: 319.

Tochmarc Emire

Hamel, A. G. van, ed. *Compert Con Culainn and Other Stories*. Mediaeval and Modern Irish Series 3. Dublin: Dublin Institute for Advanced Studies, 1933.

Meyer, Kuno ed. and trans. "The Oldest Version of Tochmarc Emire." *Revue Celtique* 11 (1890): 433–457.

Aided Derb Forgaill

Ingridsdotter, Kicki, ed. and trans. "Aided Derb Forgaill 'The Violent Death of Derb Forgaill': A Critical Edition with Introduction, Translation, and Textual Notes." PhD diss., Uppsala University, 2009. http://uu.diva-portal.org/smash/record.jsf?searchId=2&pid=diva2:213892. Last accessed April 4, 2023.

Serglige Con Culainn

Dillon, Myles, ed. *Serglige Con Culainn*. Mediaeval and Modern Irish Series 14. Dublin: Dublin Institute for Advanced Studies, 1953.

Fomin, Maxim, ed. and trans. "Bríatharthecosc Con Culainn in the Context of Early Irish Wisdom-Literature." In *Ulidia 2: Proceedings of the Second International Conference on the Ulster Cycle of Tales*, edited by Ruairí Ó hUiginn and Brian Ó Cathái. Maynooth: An Sagart, 2009: 140–172.

Gantz, Jeffrey, trans. *Early Irish Myths and Sagas*. Harmondsworth: Penguin, 1981: 153–178.

BIBLIOGRAPHIES, DATABASES, AND REFERENCE WORKS

Bibliography of Irish Linguistics and Literature. 4 vols. Ongoing. Dublin: School of Celtic Studies, Dublin Institute for Advanced Studies, 1913–. https://bill. celt.dias.ie/. Accessed June 29, 2023.

CELT: Corpus of Electronic Texts. National University of Ireland, Cork. 1997–2021. https://celt.ucc.ie/. Accessed June 28, 2023.

CODECS: Collaborative Online Database and e-Resources for Celtic Studies published by the A. G. van Hamel Foundation for Celtic Studies. https://codecs.vanhamel.nl/Home. Accessed June 28, 2023.

Hogan, Edmund. *Onomasticon Goedelicum: locorum et tribuum Hiberniae et Scotiae/An index, with identifications, to the Gaelic names of places and tribes.* Hodges, Figgis & Company, Dublin, in 1910. Reissued by Four Courts Press, Dublin, in 1993. Published online by National University of Ireland, Cork, as part of the LOCUS project. https://www.ucc.ie/en/locus/. Accessed June 28, 2023. The Onomasticon is being slowly replaced by a new *Historical Dictionary of Irish Place- and Tribal Names.* https://www.ucc.ie/en/locus/. Accessed June 29, 2023.

ISOS: Irish Script on Screen. School of Celtic Studies, Dublin Institute for Advanced Studies. Dublin. 1999–. https://www.isos.dias.ie. Accessed June 28, 2023.

SUGGESTIONS FOR

FURTHER READING

Bitel, Lisa M. *Land of Women: Tales of Sex and Gender from Early Ireland*. Ithaca, NY: Cornell University Press, 1996.

Deane, Seamus, Andrew Carpenter, and Jonathan Williams. *The Field Day Anthology of Irish Writing*. London: Field Day Publications; distributed by Faber & Faber, 1991–2002. Vol. 1: *Early and Middle Irish Literature (c. 600–1600)*.

Findon, Joanne. *A Woman's Words: Emer and Female Speech in the Ulster Cycle*. Toronto: University of Toronto Press, 1997.

Gaiman, Neil. *Norse Mythology*. New York: W. W. Norton & Company. 2018.

Kinsella, Thomas. *The Táin*. Oxford: Oxford University Press, 1985.

Mac Cana, Proinsias. *Celtic Mythology*. London: Chancellor, 1970.

Nagy, Joseph Falaky, ed. *Writing Down the Myths*. Turnhout Belgium: Brepols, 2013.

Ní Bhrolcháin, Muireann. *An Introduction to Early Irish Literature*. 17th ed. Dublin: Four Courts Press, 2019.

Ó Cróinín, Dáibhí. *Early Medieval Ireland 400–1200*. 2nd ed. Abingdon Oxon: Routledge, an imprint of the Taylor & Francis Group, 2017.

Story Archaeology: Conversations on Irish Mythology. Podcast. http://Storyarchaeology.com. Accessed July 21, 2023.

Stout, Matthew. *Early Medieval Ireland: 431–1169.* Dublin: Wordwell, 2017.

Tulsk Action Group CLG. *Rathcroghan Visitor Centre.* https://www.rathcroghan.ie/. Accessed July 21, 2023.

Williams, M. A. *Ireland's Immortals: A History of the Gods of Irish Myth.* Princeton, NJ: Princeton University Press, 2016.